APPLE W

MW01609686

SERIES 9

Complete User Manual

A Comprehensive Practical Guide with Tips and Tricks to Master
the New Apple Watch Series 9 and WatchOS 10

Robby A. Walsh

CONTENTS

Introduction

The Apple Watch Series 9 was introduced in September 2023 as the successor to the Apple Watch Series 8, which was initially released in 2015.

The Apple Watch Series 9 retains the same external design as its predecessor, with the same features and sensors. However, there are new internal developments. The 41mm and 45mm case sizes remain available, and the same rounded edges, slim-bordered display, sapphire crystal back, and Digital Crown with haptic feedback are present.

Always-On display allows users to view the watch face and complications at all times, and the display is now brighter than before. The maximal brightness is now 2000 nits, which is double the brightness of the Series 9 and makes the display more recigte in sunlight. For dark environments and at night, the display can be dimmed to one nit while remaining legible.

The Series 9 has front glass that is resistant to cracks, IP6X dust resistance, and WR50 water resistance. Wallet app-stored credit and debit cards can be used to make Apple Pay purchases, and the device has the same rapid charging capabilities as its predecessor.

The new S9 chip in the Series 9 is significantly faster than the S8 processor in the previous model and enables functionality.

Despite its new capabilities, the S9 chip's 4-core Neural Engine processes machine learning tasks up to twice as quickly, and it is more efficient for the same all-day battery life.

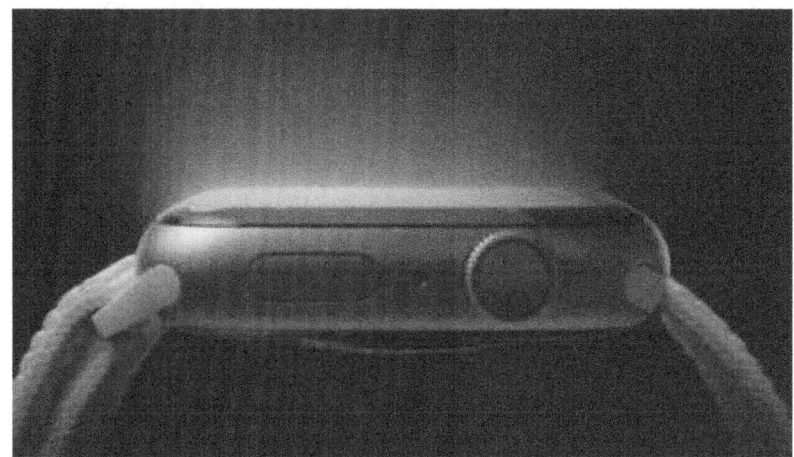

Double Tap is the most significant new capability enabled by the S9 processor. The gesture enables users to interact with the Apple Watch with one hand by tapping the index finger and thumb together. Double Tap can stop a timer, play/pause music, answer or terminate a call, and snooze an alarm, among other things.

Siri commands that do not require internet access are processed locally on the S9 for speedier response times and greater privacy, and dictation is 25 percent more accurate. In addition to asking Siri about Health app data, users can inquire about Activity progress, pulse rate, sleep, and medications.

Continually accessible features include heart rate monitoring, blood oxygen detection, ECG readings, sleep tracking, fall detection, harsh noise monitoring, and built-in temperature sensing. All of these features were introduced with previous-generation Apple products.

A Crash Detection feature uses the watch's gyroscope and accelerometer in conjunction with a sophisticated sensor-fusion algorithm to detect severe vehicle accidents and notify emergency services. In the event of a collision, the Apple Watch contacts emergency personnel if the user does not respond within 10 seconds.

With Low Power Mode, the battery life can be extended to 36 hours from the standard 18 hours. Low Power Mode disables Always-On display, heart rate measurements in the background, WiFi and cellular connections, and more.

Apple added an Ultra-Wideband processor of the second generation to the Series 9. The UWB chip facilitates Precision Finding, which provides visual, haptic, and audible guidance for locating a misplaced iPhone. Additionally, integration with HomePod has been enhanced, and when an Apple Watch is within four meters of a HomePod that is playing audio, the Series 9 can display the Now Playing interface for controlling media.

The Series 9 Apple Watch is offered in aluminum and stainless steel. The aluminum models are available in Pink, Starlight, Midnight, Silver, and (PRODUCT)RED, whereas the stainless steel variants are available in Silver, Graphite, and Gold. Along with the Series 9, Apple has introduced new band colors and materials, eradicating leather options.

Chapter 1

Set up and pair your Apple Watch with iPhone

For use with watchOS 9, you must pair your Apple Watch with an iPhone 8 or later operating iOS 16 or later. The setup assistants on your iPhone and Apple Watch collaborate to assist you in pairing and configuring your Apple Watch.

VoiceOver or Zoom can assist you in viewing your Apple Watch or iPhone, even during setup.

Before using your Apple Watch, please review the Important safety information for Apple Watch to avoid injury.

Turn on your Apple Watch, pair it, and configure it.

1. The Apple Watch should be worn on the forearm. You can adjust the band's size or the band itself so that your Apple Watch fits securely but comfortably on your wrist.
2. Apple Watch: Press and hold the side button until the Apple logo appears.
3. Bring your iPhone near to your Apple Watch, wait for the pairing screen to appear, and then tap Continue.
   Alternatively, you can launch the Apple Watch app on your iPhone and then tap Pair New Watch.

4. Tap Configure for Myself.

5. When prompted, adjust your iPhone so that your Apple Watch appears in the viewfinder of the Apple Watch app. This combines the two elements.

6. Follow the configuration instructions on your iPhone and Apple Watch after selecting Set Up Apple Watch.

   While your Apple Watch is synchronizing, tap Get to Know Your Watch to learn more about it. On your iPhone, you can discover what's new, view Apple Watch tips, and peruse this user manual. After setting up your Apple Watch, you can access this information by launching the Apple Watch app on your iPhone and selecting Discover.

Turn on mobile service

During Apple Watch setup, you can enable cellular service. If you change your mind, you can turn it on later in the Apple Watch app on your iPhone.

Both your iPhone and Apple Watch must use the same cellular service provider. However, if you set up an Apple Watch for a family member, the watch can use a separate cellular carrier than the iPhone you use to manage it.

Cellular service is not available everywhere.

Not getting along?

- If you attempt pairing and see a watch face, your Apple Watch is already paired with an iPhone. Before resetting your Apple Watch's settings, you must remove all content from it.
- If the camera fails to initiate the pairing procedure, select Pair Apple Watch. at the bottom of the iPhone's screen, then follow the on-screen instructions.
- Unpair Apple Watch if it cannot communicate to your iPhone.

Disconnect Apple Watch

1. On your iPhone, launch the Apple Watch application.
2. select My Watch, then select All Watches at the screen's top.
3. Tap ⓘ the Apple Watch you wish to unpair, followed by Unpair Apple Watch.

Multiple Apple Watches may be connected.

You can connect a second Apple Watch in the same manner as the initial connection. Bring your iPhone near to your Apple Watch, wait for the pairing screen to appear on your iPhone, and then tap the Pair button. Or, do the following:

1. On your iPhone, launch the Apple Watch application.
2. select My Watch, then select All Watches at the screen's top.
3. Tap "Add Watch," then follow the on-screen instructions.

Quickly switch to a separate Apple Watch.

When your iPhone detects your associated Apple Watch, it automatically connects to it. Place a separate Apple Watch on your wrist and raise it.

You can also customize your Apple Watch.

1. On your iPhone, launch the Apple Watch application.
2. select My Watch, then select All Watches at the screen's top.

Turn off Auto Switch.

Touch and hold the bottom of the watch's display, swipe up to open Control Center, and then search for the Connected status icon to determine whether your Apple Watch is connected to your iPhone.

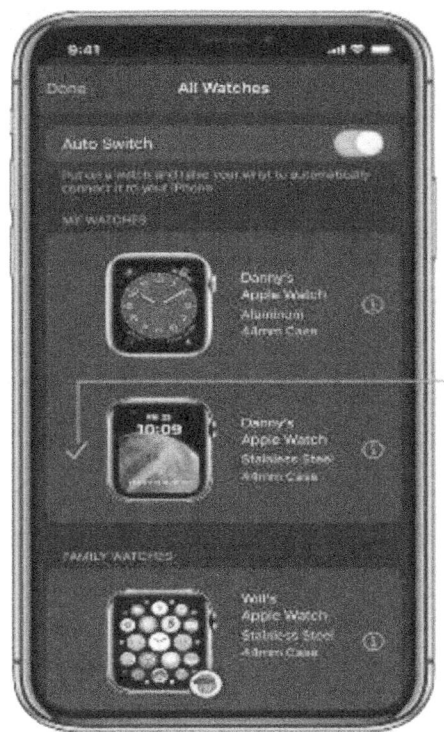

The active Apple Watch.

Connect an Apple Watch to a new iPhone.

If your old iPhone is already connected with your Apple Watch and you wish to pair it with your new iPhone, please follow the steps below:

1. Use iCloud Backup to back up the iPhone paired with your Apple Watch.
2. Assemble your new iPhone. On the Apps & Data screen, choose to restore from an iCloud backup and then select the most recent backup.
3. Continue setting up your new iPhone, and when prompted, choose to pair it with your Apple Watch.

When you are finished configuring your new iPhone, your Apple Watch will prompt you to synchronize it. Tap Accept on your Apple Watch, followed by entering its passcode.

A new Apple Watch can be added to an existing cell phone contract.

Follow these instructions to transfer your current cellular plan from one Apple Watch with cellular to another.

1. Wear your Apple Watch and utilize your iPhone to launch the Apple Watch application.

2. Go to My Watch, tap Cellular, and then tap ⓘ next to the plan you want to use.

3. Tap Remove [carrier's name] Plan, and then affirm your selection.

   You may need to contact your carrier if you wish to remove this Apple Watch from your mobile phone plan.

4. Put on your other Apple Watch with cellular, remove your old watch, tap My Watch, then tap Cellular.

Follow the instructions below to enable cellular on your watch.

The Apple Watch application

Using the Apple Watch app on your iPhone, you can alter the watch face, adjust settings and notifications, configure the Dock, and install apps, among other things.

Launch the Apple Watch application.

1. Tap the icon for the Apple Watch app on your iPhone.

2. Tap "My Watch" to view the configuration of your Apple Watch.

If you have connected multiple Apple Watches to your iPhone, you will see the settings for the one that is being used at the moment.

Swipe to see your watch face collection.

Settings for Apple Watch.

Feed your Apple Watch.

Place the charger in position

1. Place your charger and charging cable on a horizontal surface in a well-ventilated area.

1. Your Apple Watch comes with either the Apple Watch Magnetic Fast Charger to USB-C Cable (only for Apple Watch Series 7 and Apple Watch Series 8) or the Apple Watch Magnetic Charging Cable (other models). Additionally, you can use an Apple Watch Magnetic Charging Dock or a MagSafe Duo Charger (sold separately).

2. Connect the power cable to the dedicated power adapter.

3. Connect the adapter to a power source.

Not everywhere offers rapid recharge.

Start charging Apple Watch.

Place the Apple Watch Magnetic Fast Charger to USB-C cable or the Apple Watch Magnetic Charging Cable (included with Apple Watch Series 7 and later models) on the rear of your Apple Watch. The rear of your Apple Watch is magnetic, so the cup-shaped end of the charging cable snaps onto it and keeps it in the correct position.

If your Apple Watch is not in silent mode, a chime will sound and a charging symbol will appear on the watch display when charging begins. When Apple Watch requires charge, a red symbol appears. When Apple Watch is being charged, the icon turns green. In Low Power Mode, the Apple Watch charging symbol is purple.

The Apple Watch can be charged on its side or flat with the band exposed.

- Place your Apple Watch on the dock when using the Apple Watch Magnetic Charging Dock or the MagSafe Duo Charger.
- If your battery is extremely low, you may see an image of the Apple Watch Magnetic Fast Charger to USB-C Cable or Apple Watch Magnetic Charging Cable, as well as a low battery icon ⚡, on the screen.

The Series 8 Apple Watch

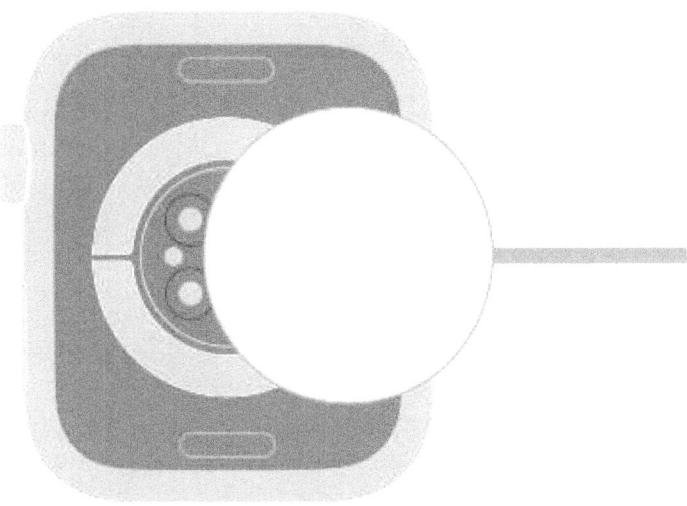

Apple Watch SE, second generation

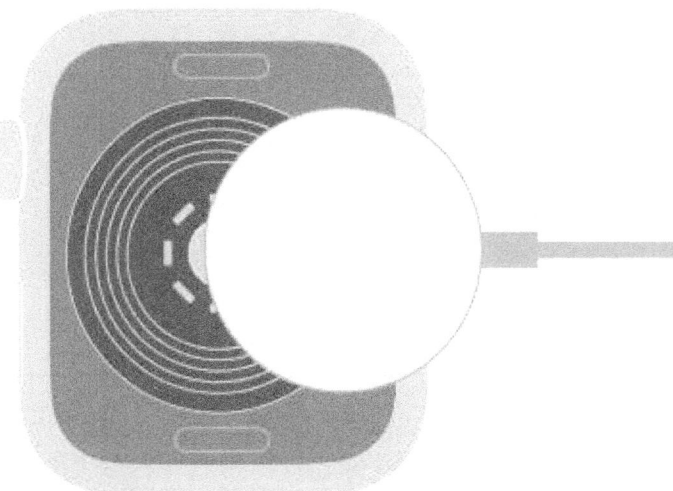

The Series 7 Apple Watch

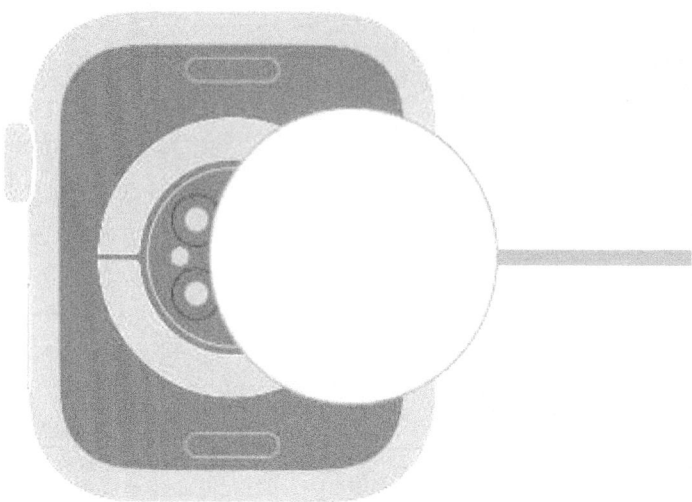

Series 6 of the Apple Watch was released in September 2018.

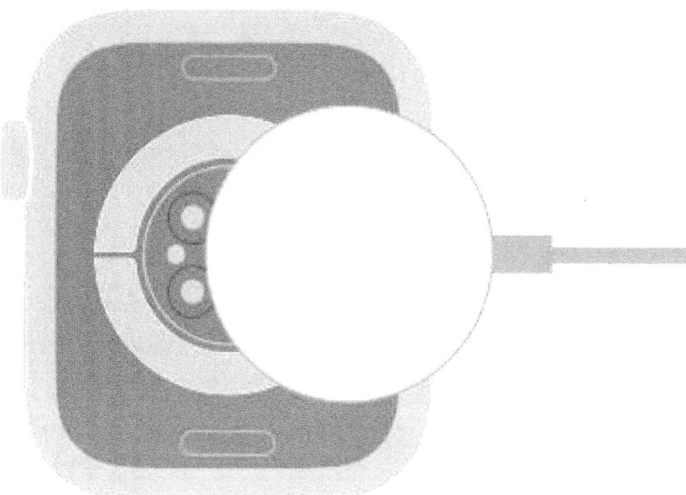

Apple's Watch SE

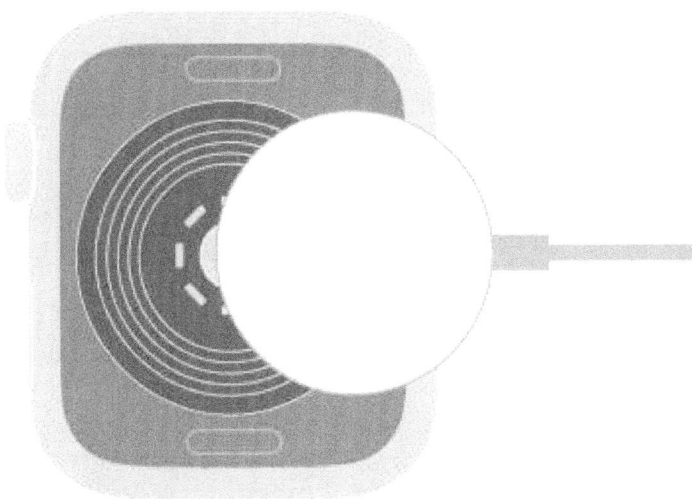

Apple's Watch 4 and Apple's Watch 5

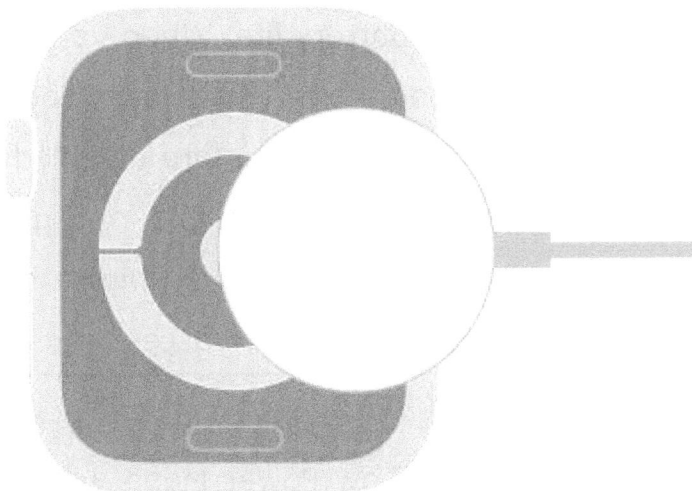

Determine how much energy remains.

Touch and hold the bottom of the display, then move up to access the Control Center and view the remaining battery life. Add a battery complication to the watch face to rapidly determine how much power remains.

View the percentage of remaining battery life.

Save energy

Low Power Mode allows you to conserve battery life. When you do so, the Always-On Display, background heart rate and blood oxygen measurements, and heart rate notifications are disabled. Other alerts might be late, emergency alerts might not get through, and some cellular and Wi-Fi connections might be limited. Until you need it, such as when you want to access music or send a text message, cellular is disabled.

When the battery reaches 80% charge, Low Power Mode will be disabled.

1. Touching and holding the screen, then swiping up to open Control Center.

2. Touch the remaining battery percentage, and then activate Low Power Mode.

3. Scroll down and select Enable Low Power Mode to validate your selection.

You can select On for 1 Day, On for 2 Days, or On for 3 Days by tapping Turn On For.

If battery-powered devices, such as AirPods, are connected to your Apple Watch via Bluetooth, their remaining charge will be displayed on this screen.

When the battery charge on your Apple Watch falls below 10 percent, you are notified and given the option to transition to Low Power Mode.

Return to the standard power mode.

1. Touching and holding the screen, then swiping up to open Control Center.

2. Tap the remaining battery percentage, and then disable Low Power Mode.

Determine how much time has passed since the last charge.

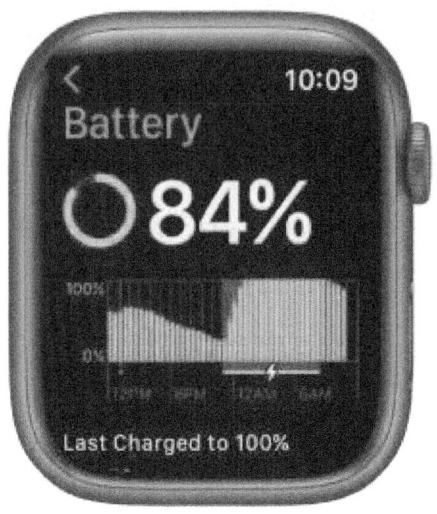

1. On the Apple Watch, launch the Settings application .

2. Tap "Battery."

On the Battery screen, you can view the remaining battery life, a graph depicting how the battery has been charged recently, and the date of the last battery charge.

Check the health of the battery.

Determine the battery capacity of your Apple Watch when it was brand new.

1. On the Apple Watch, launch the Settings application .

2. Select "Battery," followed by "Battery Health."

Apple Watch will notify you when the battery is nearly empty, allowing you to evaluate your service options.

Do not update applications in the background.

When you transition to a different application, the previous application does not remain open or consume system resources. However, it may still "refresh" in the background, meaning it may search for new and updated content.

Apps that automatically update themselves in the background can consume energy. You can disable this feature to maximize your battery life.

1. On the Apple Watch, launch the Settings application .
2. Click "General" followed by "Background App Refresh."
3. Turn off background app refresh to prevent all applications from needing to refresh. Alternatively, you may navigate down and disable refresh for each app.

Apps with complications on the current watch face will continue to update regardless of the background app refresh configuration.

Turn on and activate the Apple Watch

Turn on and off your Apple Watch.

- **Turn on:** If your Apple Watch is off, press and hold the side button until the Apple logo appears (you may see a brief blank screen beforehand).
  When Apple Watch is activated, the watch face appears.

- **Turn off:** If you need to turn off your Apple Watch, press and hold the side button until the sliders appear, then tap at the upper right and slide the Power Off slider to the right. You can view the time when your Apple Watch is off by squeezing and holding the Digital Crown.

While the Apple Watch is charging, it cannot be turned off. To power off your Apple Watch, you must first remove it from its charger.

Never End

Always On enables compatible Apple Watches to display the watch face and time even when the wrist is down. Apple Watch is completely functional when the wrist is raised.

Always On is disabled while the Apple Watch is in Low Power Mode. Tap the display to display the watch face.

Always On is available on Series 5, Series 6, Series 7, and Series 8 Apple Watches.

1. On the Apple Watch, launch the Settings application .
2. select Display & Brightness, and then select Always On to turn on the display permanently.
3. touch Always On, then touch the following settings to configure them:

- Select complications that display information when the wrist is lowered, and then select "Show Complication Data."
- Show Notifications: Select which alerts to display when you place your wrist down.
- Show applications: Select which applications to display when the wrist is down.

Start the display on the Apple Watch.

You can activate the screen of an Apple Watch in the following ways by default:

- Raise your forearm. When you rest your wrist, the Apple Watch returns to slumber.
- Press the Digital Crown button or tap on the display.

- Activate the Digital Crown.

Open the Settings app 🔘 on your Apple Watch, navigate to Display & Brightness, and disable Wake on Wrist Raise and Wake on Crown Rotation.

Use the theater mode to prevent your Apple Watch from awakening when you elevate your wrist temporarily.

If your Apple Watch does not activate when you elevate your wrist, ensure that you've selected the correct orientation for your wrist and watch. If tapping the screen or pressing or turning the Digital Crown does not activate your Apple Watch, it may need to be charged.

Back to the clock's face.

You can choose how long Apple Watch waits before closing an app and returning to the clock face.

1. On the Apple Watch, launch the Settings application 🔘 .
2. Go to General > Return to Clock, then scroll down and select Always, After 2 minutes, or After an hour for the Apple Watch to return to the clock face.
3. You can also press the Digital Crown to go return to the clock face.

By default, the setting you select affects all applications, but you can customize the time for each app if desired. Tap an app on this screen, select Custom, and then select a configuration.

Wake up and complete your final task.

You can configure Apple Watch to return you to where you were in certain applications before it went to slumber. This list includes the applications Audiobooks, Maps, Mindfulness, Music, Now Playing, Podcasts, Stopwatch, Timers, Voice Memos, Walkie-Talkie, and Workout.

1. On the Apple Watch, launch the Settings application.
2. Tap an app, then enable Return to App by navigating to Settings > General > Return to Clock, scrolling down and tapping the app.

Stop your current app activity to return to the clock face. Stop a podcast, terminate a route in Maps, or cancel a timer, for instance.

Additionally, you can launch the Apple Watch application on your iPhone, select My Watch, and then navigate to General > Return to Clock.

Keep the Apple Watch display on for an extended duration.

When you touch your Apple Watch to wake it up, you can keep the screen on for longer.

1. On the Apple Watch, launch the Settings application .
2. Select Display & Brightness, then tap Wake Duration, followed by Wake for 70 Seconds.

Locking or unlocking the Apple Watch

Unlock the iPhone watch

You can manually input the passcode to unlock Apple Watch, or you can configure it to unlock automatically when your iPhone is unlocked.

- Enter the code: After awakening the Apple Watch, enter the passcode.
- If you unlock your iPhone, you can also activate your Apple Watch: On your iPhone, open the Apple Watch app, tap My Watch, tap Passcode, and then toggle Unlock with iPhone.

To unlock your Apple Watch, your iPhone must be within the normal Bluetooth range of approximately 33 feet (10 meters). If Bluetooth is disabled on Apple Watch, you will be required to input a passcode to access it.

The passcode for your Apple Watch may differ from that of your iPhone. In fact, it is preferable to use unique passcodes.

Modify your password

To alter the passcode you created when you first set up your Apple Watch, follow these steps:

1. On the Apple Watch, launch the Settings application .
2. Tap "Passcode," then tap "Change Passcode," and then adhere to the on-screen instructions.

Additionally, you can open the Apple Watch app on your iPhone, tap My Watch, tap Passcode, press Change Password, and then follow the on-screen instructions.

To use a passcode consisting of more than four digits, open the Settings app on your Apple Watch, select Passcode, and then deactivate Simple Passcode.

Avoid using the code.

1. On the Apple Watch, launch the Settings application .
2. Select "Passcode," followed by "Turn Passcode Off."

You can also launch the Apple Watch application on your iPhone, tap My Watch, tap Passcode, and then tap Turn Passcode Off.

Note: If you disable your passcode on your Apple Watch, you cannot use Apple Pay.

Automatically Lock

When you remove your Apple Watch, it will automatically lock by default. Change the following settings to modify wrist detection.

1. On the Apple Watch, launch the Settings application .

2. Tap Passcode, and then toggle Wrist Detection on or off.

• When wrist detection is disabled, the following Apple Watch features are affected:

• You will be prompted for your passcode when you double-click the side icon to authorize a payment with Apple Pay on your Apple Watch.

• Certain Activity measurements are inaccessible.

• Heart rate monitoring and alerts have been disabled.

• The Apple Watch no longer automatically locks and unlocks itself.

• Even if Apple Watch detects a forceful fall, it will not automatically dial 911.

Lock manually

1. Touching and holding the screen, then swiping up to open Control Center.

2. Tap .

To manually secure your Apple Watch, you must deactivate wrist detection. Open the Settings app on your Apple Watch, select Passcode, and then disable Wrist Detection.

When you next wish to use your Apple Watch, you will be required to input your passcode.

You can also secure your screen to prevent accidental touches while exercising. Swipe right while in the Workout app on your Apple Watch, then select Lock. Water Lock automatically hides the display of your Apple Watch when you begin a swimming workout.

If you have forgotten your passphrase

If you neglect your passcode, your Apple Watch must be erased. Here are some strategies:

- Detach your Apple Watch from your iPhone in order to expunge your settings and passcode, and then re-pair.
- Reset your Apple Watch and re-pair it with your iPhone.

After ten failed attempts to activate the Apple Watch, delete it.

If your Apple Watch is lost or stolen, you can configure it to expunge all of its data after 10 incorrect passcode attempts. This safeguards your information.

1. On the Apple Watch, launch the Settings application .
2. Tap Passcode, followed by Erase Data.

Change the direction and language of Apple Watch.

26

Choose a language or region.

If you have configured your iPhone to use multiple languages, you can select which language appears on your Apple Watch.

1. On your iPhone, launch the Apple Watch application.
2. Tap "My Watch," navigate to "General" > "Language & Region," tap "Custom," and then select the desired language.

Change the way your wrists or Digital Crown are facing.

If you want to wear your Apple Watch on the other wrist or would prefer the Digital Crown to be on the opposite side, you can change your orientation settings so that raising your wrist wakes your Apple Watch and turning the Digital Crown advances the desired controls.

1. On the Apple Watch, launch the Settings application.

2. Select General > Orientation from the General menu.

You can also access the Apple Watch app on your iPhone, tap My Watch, and then go to General > Watch Orientation.

Remove, replace, and secure Apple Watch Bands

Follow these general steps to remove, replace, and reapply a band.

Ensure that the band you choose is compatible with the dimensions of your Apple Watch case. As long as the measurements are the same, you can use a band designed for Apple Watch (1st generation) or Apple Watch Series 1, 2, and 3 with Apple Watch Series 4, Apple Watch Series 5, Apple Watch SE, Apple Watch Series 6, Apple Watch Series 7, Apple Watch SE (2nd Generation), and Apple Watch Series 8. 38mm, 40mm, and 41mm bands are interchangeable with 42mm, 44mm, and 45mm bands.

The vast majority of bands designed for Apple Watch Series 4, Apple Watch Series 5, Apple Watch SE, Apple Watch Series 6,

Apple Watch Series 7, Apple Watch SE (2nd Generation), and Apple Watch Series 8 are compatible with older Apple Watch models. Apple Watch Series 4, Apple Watch Series 5, Apple Watch SE, Apple Watch Series 6, Apple Watch Series 7, Apple Watch SE (2nd Generation), and Apple Watch Series 8 are compatible with the Solo Loop and Braided Solo Loop bands. Apple Watch Series 4, Apple Watch Series 5, Apple Watch SE, Apple Watch Series 6, Apple Watch Series 7, Apple Watch SE (2nd Generation), and Apple Watch Series 8 are compatible with bands designed for earlier Apple Watch models.

Remove and change band

1. Maintain pressure on the button on your Apple Watch that allows you to remove the band.
2. Slide the band back and forth to remove it, then slide the replacement band on.

Do not attempt to force a band into position. If removing or putting on a band is difficult, click the band release button again.

Attach a strap.

For your Apple Watch to function optimally, it should fit snugly on your wrist.

The rear of your Apple Watch must contact your skin for wrist detection, haptic notifications, and the heart rate sensor to function. Wearing your Apple Watch correctly — not too tightly, not too loosely, and with space for your skin to breathe — keeps you comfortable and allows the sensors to function properly. Additionally, the sensors only function when the Apple Watch is worn on the upper forearm.

Chapter 2

Set up a family member's Apple Watch

You can set up and manage Apple Watch for someone who does not have an iPhone, such as a guardian or child who does not have a phone at school. To do so, you must be the family organizer for the group or a parent or guardian.

The iPhone used to pair and set up the Apple Watch must be within normal Bluetooth range (approximately 33 feet or 10 meters) in order to alter settings and update software. The person for whom you are configuring Apple Watch must be a member of your Family Sharing group and have an Apple Watch Series 4 or later that can communicate to a mobile phone. (The cell phone service provider for your relative's watch does not need to be the same as for your iPhone.)

Family Setup is not available in all locations.

Using the Apple Watch app and Screen Time on your iPhone, you can do the following:

- Guidelines for communication and safety
- A plan for screen breaks
- Schooltime is a feature that restricts certain Apple Watch capabilities while children are in school.
- Email and calendar settings for iCloud, Gmail, and other services

- Configurations that restrict access to explicit content, purchases, and private data

Depending on how the administered Apple Watch is configured, you can also view its Activity, Health, and Location information.

Note: An Apple Watch set up for a family member cannot perform all the functions of the iPhone on which it was set up. For instance, you cannot unlock a paired iPhone from a family member's Apple Watch, nor can you transmit tasks from the managed Apple Watch to the iPhone. If you delete an app from a family member's Apple Watch, it will not be removed from the iPhone used to set up the Apple Watch.

Configure the Apple Watch of a relative.

Setting up an Apple Watch for a relative is identical to setting one up for yourself. Before pairing and configuring a family member's watch, you should erase it to ensure that it is vacant.

1. Instruct the family member to put on their Apple Watch. Change the size of the band or adjust it so that the Apple Watch fits securely but comfortably on their wrist.
2. To switch on Apple Watch, press and hold the side button until the Apple logo appears.
3. Bring your iPhone near to your Apple Watch, wait for the pairing screen to appear, and then tap Continue.

Or, on your iPhone, launch the Apple Watch app and select "My Watch," "All Watches," and "Add Watch."

4. Tap Set Up for a Family Member, followed by Tap Continue on the subsequent screen.

5. When prompted, adjust your iPhone so that the Apple Watch appears in the viewfinder of the Apple Watch app. This combines the two elements.

6. Tap Set Apple Watch up. Follow the instructions on your iPhone and Apple Watch to complete setup.

Manage the Apple Watch of a relative.

1. Launch the Apple Watch management software on the iPhone.

2. Touch My Watch, followed by Family Watches, then a watch, and finally Done.

When you tap My Watch on a managed watch, you can modify several parameters, including:

Setting	Options
General	Check for updates, change language and region, and reset Apple Watch.
Cellular	Set up cellular if you haven't.
Accessibility	Configure accessibility settings.
Emergency SOS	Turn on or off the option to hold the side button to call emergency services, and add and change emergency contacts.
Schooltime	Set up a Schooltime schedule.
Screen Time	Manage parental controls, get insights about your family member's screen time, and set limits.
Activity	Manage a fitness experience made for younger users.
Contacts	Choose trusted contacts.
Find My	Choose notification settings.
Handwashing	Manage restrictions, and turn the handwashing timer on or off.
Health	Add or edit health details and Medical ID, view the health data (with the proper permissions and settings) of the person who uses the managed Apple Watch, request to share health data, and choose to stop receiving health data.

A managed Apple Watch does not have all the features of a manually configured Apple Watch.

Establish Screen Time

Utilize Screen Time to configure parental controls for a family member's Apple Watch. Screen Time allows you to set times when no one in your household can use a screen. You can also restrict who they can communicate with and the applications they can use to do so. You can also limit iTunes Store and app purchases, explicit content, and the device's location.

Follow the procedures below to configure Screen Time:

1. Launch the Apple Watch management software on the iPhone.
2. Touch My Watch, followed by Family Watches, then a watch, and finally Done.
3. Select Screen Time, then Screen Time Settings, followed by Screen Time On.
4. 4.On the subsequent screens, configure settings for what content is permitted, how secure communication is, how long you can be away from screens, and how long you can spend on applications and websites.
5. Set a password for Screen Time.

You can also alter Screen Time settings by opening the Settings app on your iPhone, tapping Screen Time, tapping your family member's name under the Family heading, tapping Turn On Screen Time, and then tapping alter Settings.

Schooltime can be started on your Apple Watch.

Schooltime restrictions During school hours, an Apple Watch can assist a family member with concentration.

Set a schedule for education

1. Launch the Apple Watch management software on the iPhone.
2. Touch My Watch, followed by Family Watches, and then a watch.
3. Select "Done" followed by "Schooltime."
4. Turn on Schooltime, then select Edit Schedule.
5. Select the days and times Schooltime will operate on your watch.
6. Tap "Add Time" if you wish to create multiple schedules in a single day, such as from 8:00 a.m. to 12:00 p.m. and then from 1:00 p.m. to 3:00 p.m.

Get away from education!

Your family member can temporarily abandon Schooltime, perhaps to check their activity rings.

Tap the display, press and hold the Digital Crown, and then tap the "Exit" icon.

If you abandon Schooltime during a predetermined time, the Schooltime watch face will return when you put down your wrist.

Schooltime remains inactive during non-scheduled hours until the next scheduled start time or until you tap ![icon] Control Center.

Determine when Schooltime became accessible.

When a family member departs Schooltime, you receive a report detailing the date and duration of their departure. To view the report, please follow these steps:

1. Launch the Apple Watch management software on the iPhone.
2. Touch My Watch, followed by Family Watches, and then a watch.
3. press "Done," and then press "Schooltime," to view reports of the days, times, and durations Schooltime was unlocked.

The report is also accessible via Apple Watch. Launch the Settings application ![icon] on your Apple Watch, and then select Schooltime to view it.

After the screen falls to sleep, Schooltime resumes.

If your family member has joined an after-school study group that meets outside of scheduled hours and does not wish to be interrupted, they can activate Schooltime when it is not operating. Touch and hold the bottom of the display, then swipe up and select ![icon] Control Center. To exit Schooltime, press and hold the Digital Crown, then tap Exit. When it is time or when Control Center is activated, school will resume.

Play music on a managed Apple Watch.

As long as you have a Wi-Fi or cellular connection, you can listen to Apple Music on your managed Apple Watch if you are a member of a Family Sharing group that has an Apple Music family subscription.

1. Open the Music app 🎵 on the Apple Watch you administer.
2. Perform any of the subsequent.

- Click "Listen Now" to hear music hand-selected for you based on your listening habits.
- Tap Radio to listen to Apple Music Radio and genre-specific radio stations.
- Tap "Library" to browse your Apple Watch's audio collection.
- Tap Search, then input, speak, or scribble an artist, album, or playlist's name (only on Apple Watch Series 7 and Apple Watch Series 8).
  Scribble is not supported in all languages.
- Tap a playlist created by the editors of Apple Music for children and adolescents.
- Touch the albums and playlists that you've added to your Apple Watch.

3. Utilize the controls in the Music app and the Now Playing app to play and select music.

A managed Apple Watch can add podcasts and stream them.

You can follow podcasts and listen to them directly on a managed Apple Watch.

Siri is capable of playing recordings.

Say to Siri, "Hey Siri, please play the podcast Wild Things." The most recent podcast episode is played on your Apple Watch.

Obtain a podcast to hear.

1. Launch the Podcasts application on the Apple Watch that you control.
2. Tap Search, then enter the name of a podcast before tapping the program.

Tap Follow to continue following the show. To view an episode, tap on it.

Chapter 3

See activity and health reports for family members

Once daily activity objectives have been established, a family member's daily activity level can be determined. If the individual consents, you may also view their health information.

Set objectives for a family member to complete tasks.

Move objectives for children with a manageable Apple Watch are based on minutes of movement rather than calories burned. The exercise objective is minutes of vigorous activity, such as sprinting, jumping, and playing. Outdoor run, walk, and cycling exercises are designed for children under 13 years of age.

Regardless of the family member's age, if you manage an Apple Watch for a family member, you can alter the fitness experience from under-13 to over-13.

1. Launch the Apple Watch application on the iPhone used to control the Apple Watch.
2. Touch My Watch, followed by Family Watches, and then a watch.
3. Select "Done," then select "Activity," and then turn off or on "Under 13 years old."

This can also be done by accessing the Settings app on the Apple Watch, tapping Activity, and then toggling "Under 13 years old" on or off.

Examine the activity report.

1. After setting activity objectives for a family member, launch the Health app on your iPhone.
2. Click Sharing, then click your family member's name under "Sharing with you."
3. Select Activity.
4. Tap the timeline to view your family member's activities up until the current time.

You can view activity information by the day, week, month, or year.

Investigate your heath.

If your family member has granted permission, you can view additional information about their activity, as well as their hearing health and pulse rate.

1. Launch the Health application on your iPhone, then select Sharing.
2. Click the name of your family member under "Sharing with you."
3. Select Health Categories, followed by a category.

Add health-related details and Medical ID.

If you did not enter your family member's health information when you created the account, you must do the following:

1. Launch the Apple Watch management software on the iPhone.
2. Touch My Watch, followed by Family Watches, and then a watch.
3. select Done, select Health, and then do any of the following.

- Tap Health Details to add or modify information such as your birth date, height, and weight.
- select Medical ID, then select Edit to add emergency contacts and additional information.

Health information and Medical ID can be displayed on both the iPhone used to control the Apple Watch and the watch itself.

- Launch the Health app on your iPhone, select Sharing, tap the family member's name, and then select Profile.

- On the managed Apple Watch, launch the Settings app and then select Health.

Use Apple Cash Family on a family member's Apple Watch.

If you administer a Family Sharing group, you can configure Apple Cash so that children and teenagers in your group can use their Apple Watches to make purchases and send and receive money via Messages. You can also restrict who your child can send money to, receive transaction alerts, or freeze their account.

Apple Cash is not available everywhere and is only compatible with the iPhone SE, iPhone 6, and later variants.

Organize Apple Cash Family

To set up Apple Cash Family, you must be the family organizer, and the family members you wish to set up Apple Cash for must be under 18 years old.

1. On your iPhone, navigate to Settings > [your name] > Family Sharing.
2. 2.tap Apple Cash, then select an infant or adolescent.
3. Select Set Up Apple Cash and then follow the on-screen instructions to establish the account.

Your relative can send, receive, and request money in the United States, and they can also use Apple Pay to make purchases.

Apple Cash can be managed on a family member's Apple Watch.

1. Launch the Wallet app on the iPhone connected to the watch.
2. Touch your Apple Cash card, followed by the icon.
3. Select a name from the Family section.
4. Configure the following options:
- Indicate to your family member who they can give money to.
- Choose to be notified when a family member acquires or sells an item.
5. Click "Send Money" to launch the Messages app and transmit money using Apple Pay.

To prevent a family member from using Apple Pay or the Messages app to send or receive money, tap Lock Apple Cash.

To view a family member's purchases, tap Transactions on this screen or open the Wallet app on your iPhone and touch your Apple Cash card. When you select Recent Transactions or Transactions in [year], you can view the activities of your family members.

Chapter 4

Open apps on Apple Watch

You can launch any Apple Watch app from the Home Screen. The Dock makes it simple to access frequently used applications. You can store up to ten of your preferred applications in the Dock.

You can display your applications as a grid or a list.

On the Home Screen, apps can be displayed as a grid or a list. Follow the instructions below to select:

1. Press and hold the Home button.
2. Choose either List View or Grid View.

Use the Home Screen to launch applications.

The view selected impacts how an application is launched.

- Tap the application icon to display the grid view. If you are already on the Home Screen, you can rotate the Digital Crown to launch the app in the center of the display.

From the watch face, press to see the Home Screen.

Tap to open an app.

- To view a list, rotate the Digital Crown and tap an application.

Turn the Digital Crown to browse the apps.

Tap to open an app.

Press the Digital Crown once to return from an app to the Home Screen, and press it again to alter the watch face (or tap the Home Screen in grid view).

While viewing another app or the watch face, double-click the Digital Crown to rapidly open the most recently used app.

Start an application from the Dock

1. Press the side trigger and rotate the Digital Crown to navigate the Dock's applications.
2. To launch an app, tap it.

Turn the Digital Crown to see more apps. Tap one to open it.

You can choose which applications appear in the Dock.

You can choose to display up to 10 of your preferred applications or the most recently used applications in the Dock.

- To view the most recently used apps, access the Settings app on your Apple Watch, select Dock, and then select Recents. The most recently used app is displayed at the top of the Dock, followed by the other applications in reverse chronological order of their last use.

   You can use your iPhone as well. Launch the Apple Watch app, then select My Watch, Dock, and Recents.

- To view your favorite apps, open the Apple Watch app on your iPhone, touch My Watch, and then tap Dock. select Favorites, followed by Edit, and then select the applications you wish to add. Rearrange the items by dragging them around. When finished, touch Done.
- To remove an application from the Dock, select the side button and move the Digital Crown to the desired application. Swipe the application to the left, then tap the X icon.

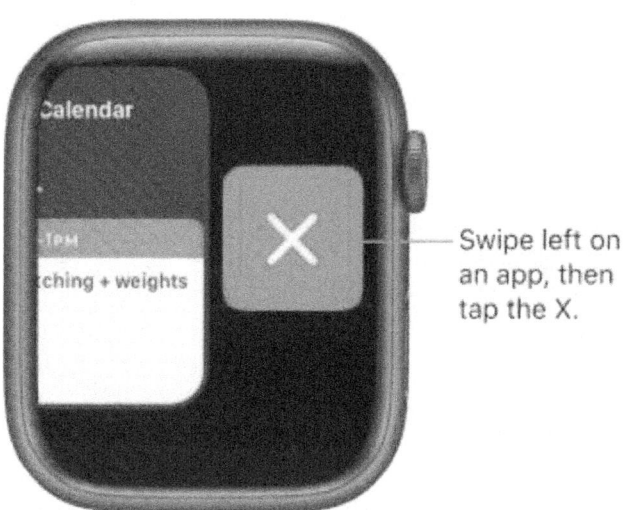

Swipe left on an app, then tap the X.

- To switch from the Dock to the Home Screen, navigate to the bottom of the Dock and tap All Apps.

Note: Apps presently running a session, such as a Maps navigation session or a Workout session, always appear at the top of the list of apps, regardless of whether Recents or Favorites is selected.

Apple Watch customers can obtain additional apps.

Apps on your Apple Watch can assist you in communicating, monitoring your health and fitness, and keeping track of the time. You can also install existing third-party applications on your iPhone, and you can download new apps from the App Store on either your iPhone or Apple Watch. On the Home Screen, you will find all of your applications.

Note: If you add an app to your Apple Watch and enable Automatic Downloads in Settings > App Store > Automatic Downloads, the iOS version will automatically download. Ensure that Automatic Updates is also enabled to obtain the most recent versions of your Apple Watch applications.

Apple Watch permits the download of programs from the App Store.

1. Open the App Store app on the Apple Watch.
2. Turn the Digital Crown to browse featured applications. To view additional apps, select a category or "See All" beneath a group.
3. Tap Get for a free app download. Tap the app's price to purchase it.

It indicates that you've already purchased the app and can obtain it again for free. Certain applications require the iOS version of the program on your iPhone.

Tap the Search field at the top of the display, then type (only on Apple Watch Series 7 and later) or use dictation or Scribble to input the app's name. You can also select a category to view the most popular apps at the moment.

When using Apple Watch with cellular, you may be required to pay for cellular data. Not all languages are supported by Scribble.

Install applications that you already own on your iPhone.

Apps on your iPhone that are compatible with watchOS are automatically installed and displayed on the Home Screen. Follow these procedures to install only specific applications:

1. On your iPhone, launch the Apple Watch application.
2. Select "My Watch," followed by "General," then "Automatic App Install."
3. Touch My Watch and then touch Available Apps.
4. Tap Install next to the apps you wish to install.

Apple Watch customers can obtain additional apps.

Apps on your Apple Watch can assist you in communicating, monitoring your health and fitness, and keeping track of the time. You can also install existing third-party applications on your iPhone, and you can download new apps from the App Store on either your iPhone or Apple Watch. On the Home Screen, you will find all of your applications.

Note: If you add an app to your Apple Watch and enable Automatic Downloads in Settings > App Store > Automatic Downloads, the iOS version will automatically download. Ensure that Automatic Updates is also enabled to obtain the most recent versions of your Apple Watch applications.

Apple Watch permits the download of programs from the App Store.

1. Open the App Store app on the Apple Watch.
2. 2.Turn the Digital Crown to browse featured applications. To view additional apps, select a category or "See All" beneath a group.
3. Tap Get for a free app download. Tap the app's price to purchase it.

It indicates that you've already purchased the app and can obtain it again for free. Certain applications require the iOS version of the program on your iPhone.

Tap the Search field at the top of the display, then type (only on Apple Watch Series 7 and later) or use dictation or Scribble to input the app's name. You can also select a category to view the most popular apps at the moment.

When using Apple Watch with cellular, you may be required to pay for cellular data. Not all languages are supported by Scribble.

Install applications that you already own on your iPhone.

Apps on your iPhone that are compatible with watchOS are automatically installed and displayed on the Home Screen. Follow these procedures to install only specific applications:

1. On your iPhone, launch the Apple Watch application.

2. Select "My Watch," followed by "General," then "Automatic App Install."
3. Touch My Watch and then touch Available Apps.
4. Tap Install next to the apps you wish to install.

Timekeeping on Apple Watch

Your Apple Watch displays the time in multiple ways.

- Lift your forearm up. The time will be displayed on the watch face, within the clock in grid view, and in the upper-right corner of the majority of applications.

- To hear the time, open the Settings app on your Apple Watch, select Clock, and then enable Speak Time. For the time to be audible, place two fingers on the watch face.

- Apple Watch can also emit a chime on the hour. Tap Clock in the Settings app of Apple Watch, then enable Chimes. Choose between Birds and Bells by selecting Sounds.

- Feel the time: When your Apple Watch is in silent mode, you can tap out the time by opening the Settings app, tapping Clock, tapping Taptic Time, turning on Taptic Time, and then selecting an option.

- If Taptic Time is disabled, Apple Watch may be set to always display the time. To enable Taptic Time, navigate to Settings > Clock > Speak Time > Control with Silent Mode.

- Raise your wrist and say "What time is it?" to activate Siri.

The Apple Watch displays status icons.

The status indicators at the top of the screen contain information about your Apple Watch.

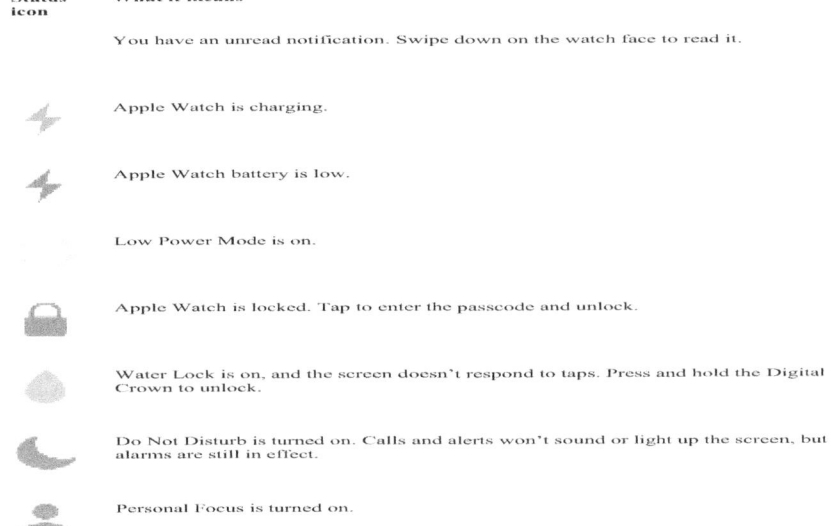

Status icon	What it means
	You have an unread notification. Swipe down on the watch face to read it.
⚡	Apple Watch is charging.
⚡	Apple Watch battery is low.
	Low Power Mode is on.
🔒	Apple Watch is locked. Tap to enter the passcode and unlock.
💧	Water Lock is on, and the screen doesn't respond to taps. Press and hold the Digital Crown to unlock.
🌙	Do Not Disturb is turned on. Calls and alerts won't sound or light up the screen, but alarms are still in effect.
👤	Personal Focus is turned on.

Utilize the Apple Watch Control Center

Control Center makes it simple to check your battery, mute your watch, select a Focus, transform your Apple Watch into a flashlight, place it in airplane mode, and activate theater mode, among other functions.

Start or stop Control Center

- To access the Control Center, swipe up the watch face. Touch and hold the bottom of another screen, then swipe upwards.

Note: Control Center cannot be accessed from the Apple Watch's Home Screen. Instead, press the Digital Crown to access the watch face or an application, then press it again to access the Control Center.

To dismiss the Control Center, swipe down from the top of the screen or press the Digital Crown.

con	Description
((ᵠ))	Turn cellular on or off—Apple Watch models with cellular only.
📶	Disconnect from Wi-Fi.
🖐	Turn on Schooltime—managed Apple Watch models only.
((☐))	Ping your iPhone.
	Check your battery percentage.
	Silence Apple Watch.
	Lock your watch with a passcode.
	Turn on theater mode.
	Make yourself available for Walkie-Talkie.
	Choose a Focus/Do Not Disturb.

Check Status of Control Center

The indicators at the top of Control Center indicate the status of the majority of Apple Watch settings. A series of small indicators may indicate, for instance, that your Apple Watch is connected to your iPhone, that Airplane mode is active, and that an application has requested your location.

To learn more, tap the group of icons at the top of Control Center.

Move the Control Center location.

To alter the order of the buttons in the Control Center, follow these steps:

1. 1.To access Control Center, tap and hold the bottom of the display, then swipe up.
2. Tap Edit at the bottom of the Control Center.
3. Touch and hold an icon before dragging it to a different location.
4. When finished, touch Done.

Remove the Control Center controls

Follow these procedures to remove Control Center's buttons:

1. To access Control Center, tap and hold the bottom of the display, then swipe up.
2. Tap Edit at the bottom of the Control Center.
3. Tap the button's corner where it should be removed.
4. When finished, touch Done.

To restore a removed button, launch Control Center, select Edit, and then tap the button in the corner. When finished, touch Done.

Change to airplane mode.

If your Apple Watch and iPhone are in "airplane mode," certain airlines will allow you to fly with them on. Bluetooth remains active while Wi-Fi and cellular (on Apple Watch models with cellular) are disabled when airport mode is activated. You can alter which settings are active and inactive when you activate airplane mode.

- To activate the aircraft mode on your Apple Watch, touch and hold the bottom of the screen, swipe up to open the Control Center, and then tap.

- Say something similar to "Turn on airplane mode" to Siri.

- You can place both your Apple Watch and iPhone into airplane mode in a single step by opening the Apple Watch app on your iPhone, tapping My Watch, navigating to General > Airplane Mode, and then activating Mirror iPhone. When your iPhone and Apple Watch are within normal Bluetooth range of each other (approximately 33 feet or 10 meters), when you transition the iPhone to airplane mode, the Apple Watch also switches to airplane mode.

- Modify which settings are enabled or disabled when the aircraft is in flight mode: Open the Settings app on your Apple Watch, tap Airplane Mode, and then choose whether Wi-Fi and Bluetooth should be enabled or disabled by default when airplane mode is activated.

While your Apple Watch is in aircraft mode, you can activate or deactivate Wi-Fi and Bluetooth through the Settings app.

When the mobile device is in airport mode, the icon appears at the top of the screen.

Even if Mirror iPhone is enabled, you must manually disable the aircraft mode on your iPhone and Apple Watch.

Use the Apple Watch flashlight.

Without impairing your night vision, you can use the flashlight to illuminate a dark door lock, warn people when you're out for a nighttime run, or shine light on adjacent objects.

- To activate the flashlight, press and hold the bottom of the display, swipe up to access the Control Center, and then tap. Swipe left to select from a constant white light, a flickering white light, and a constant red light.
- To switch off the flashlight, press the Digital Crown or a side button, or swipe down from the top of the watch face.

Use the theater mode on the Apple Watch.

In theater mode, the Apple Watch display remains opaque when the user raises their wrist. It also enables silent mode and disables your Walkie-Talkie, but you will continue to sense haptic notifications.

Touch and hold the bottom of the display, swipe up to access the Control Center, then tap Theater Mode.

When theater mode is activated, the top of the screen is visible.

When theater mode is enabled, Apple Watch can be awoken by touching the screen, pressing the Digital Crown or side button, or rotating the Digital Crown.

Getting off of Wi-Fi

You can temporarily disengage from a Wi-Fi network and, on Apple Watch models with cellular, switch to the cellular connection from the Control Center.

Touch and hold the bottom of the display, swipe up to access Control Center, and then tap Control Center.

Your Apple Watch temporarily disconnects from the Wi-Fi network. If you have a cellular Apple Watch and are in a coverage area, the cellular connection will function. When you leave a location where you were connected to Wi-Fi and return later, your Apple Watch automatically reconnects to that network, unless you've forgotten the iPhone's password.

Touch and hold the Wi-Fi button in Control Center to rapidly access the Apple Watch's Wi-Fi settings.

Change to silent mode

Touch and hold the bottom of the screen, then swipe up to open the Control Center, followed by a tap.

Even in silent mode, your Apple Watch's alarms and timers will continue to sound while it is charging.

Additionally, you can open the Apple Watch application on your iPhone, tap My Watch, touch Sounds & Haptics, and then toggle silent mode.

When you receive an alert on your Apple Watch, you can muffle it by placing your palm on the display for at least three seconds. A touch will indicate that the mute is activated. Cover to Mute must be enabled on the Apple Watch. To accomplish this, launch the Settings application, select Sounds & Haptics, and then toggle Cover to Mute.

Locate your phone.

If your iPhone is nearby, your Apple Watch will assist you in locating it.

Touch and hold the bottom of the screen, then swipe up to open the Control Center, followed by a tap.

So that you may locate your iPhone, it emits a vibration.

Are you unsure? Touching and holding the Ping button on the iPhone causes the iPhone to illuminate.

If your iPhone is out of range from your Apple Watch, use Find My on iCloud.com.

Locate your Apple Watch.

Utilize Find My to locate your lost watch.

1. On your iOS device, launch the Find My app.
2. Tap Devices, followed by your watch's name in the list.

You can play a sound on your watch, tap Directions to receive Maps directions, mark it as lost, or delete it.

Concentrate on the Apple Watch.

When you need to concentrate on something, concentration helps you remain in the present. Focus can reduce distractions by allowing you to receive only the notifications you desire (those that match your focus) and by notifying other people and apps that you are occupied.

Focus allows you to choose between Personal, Sleep, and Work. Alternately, you can configure a custom Focus on your iPhone and choose who can contact you, which apps can send you alerts, and whether you want time-sensitive notifications.

Note: If you use the same Apple ID on multiple devices, you can share your iPhone's Focus settings by heading to Settings, tapping Focus, and then toggling Share Across Devices.

Focus is either on or off.

1. To access Control Center, tap and hold the bottom of the display, then swipe up.
2. contact and hold the current Focus button, then contact a Focus ☾.

   If Focus is not enabled, Control Center displays the Do Not Disturb icon.
3. Select a Focus option: On, On for 1 hour, On until tonight/tomorrow, or On until my departure.

To turn off the Focus, tap its icon in Control Center.

When a Focus is active, its icon appears atop the watch face, alongside the time in applications, and in Control Center.

Focus on your desires.

1. Select Settings ⚙️ > Concentrate on your iPhone.

2. Tap ➕ , select a Focus, and then adhere to the on-screen instructions.

You can give a custom focus a name and select a color and an icon to signify it when you create one.

Choose a Focus dial for your watch.

When each Focus is active, you can select a distinct watch face to display. For instance, the Apple Watch can display the Simple watch face when Work Focus is enabled.

1. Select Settings ⚙️ > Concentrate on your iPhone.
2. Tap Set Up beside an existing Focus or create a new one. select Customize Focus, then select Choose under the Apple Watch image.
3. Select a visage, then press "Done."

Create a schedule for concentration.

On Apple Watch, you have control over when each Focus begins and ends. You can even initiate a Focus at various times of day. Monday through Friday, you could set the Work Focus to begin at

9:00 AM and end at 12:00 PM. You may not have a Focus between noon and 1 p.m., or your Personal Focus may take over. The Work Focus should then resume from 1 to 5 p.m., Monday through Thursday.

1. On the Apple Watch, launch the Settings application.
2. Tap "Focus," then "Work," followed by "Add new."
3. Tap the From and To fields and type in the times you want the Focus to start and stop.
4. Choose which days the Focus will be on by scrolling down.
5. Tap in the upper-left corner to save the Focus.
6. Continue doing so to add more items to the Focus.

Remove or disable a Focus schedule

To turn off a Focus schedule or get rid of it, do one of the following:

-   To disable a Focus schedule, open the Settings app on your Apple Watch, touch Focus, and then tap a Focus. Tap a schedule, then scroll down and disable Enabled.

To restore the schedule's functionality, toggle Enabled.

- To delete a Focus, launch the Settings app 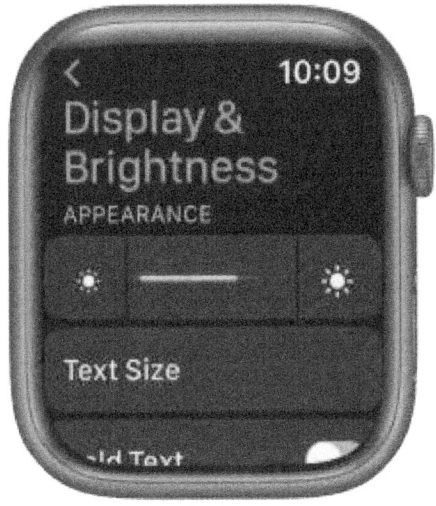 on your Apple Watch, select Focus, and then tap a Focus. select an appointment, then scroll down and select "Delete."

You can adjust the brightness, text size, audio, and haptics on Apple Watch.

Apple Watch allows you to adjust the luminance and font size.

Launch the Settings app on your Apple Watch and select Display & Brightness to make adjustments to:

- Adjust the brightness by touching the Brightness controls or the slider and rotating the Digital Crown.
- Select Text Size, then select the letters or rotate the Digital Crown to adjust the text size.
- Turn on Text in Bold if bold text is desired.

These modifications are also possible on the iPhone. Change the brightness and text by launching the Apple Watch app on your iPhone, tapping My Watch, then Display & Brightness, and then adjusting the brightness and text.

Adjust music

1. On the Apple Watch, launch the Settings application.
2. Sounds of Tapping and Touch.
3. Tap the volume controls or slider located beneath Alert Volume, and then rotate the Digital Crown to make adjustments.

Or, on your iPhone, launch the Apple Watch app, select Sounds & Haptics, and then adjust the Alert Volume slider.

Additionally, you can reduce the volume of headphones connected to your Apple Watch. In the Settings⚙ program, navigate to Sounds & Haptics > Headphone Safety and enable Reduce Loud Sounds.

Change how challenging it feels

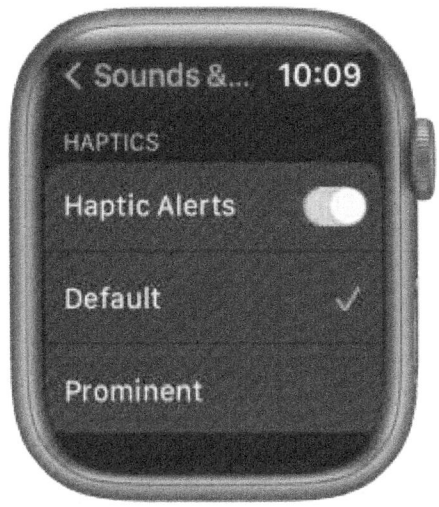

You can adjust the force with which Apple Watch jabs your wrist to notify you of notifications and alerts. This is known as haptics.

1. On the Apple Watch, launch the Settings application.
2. Tap Sounds & Haptics then activate Haptic Alerts.
3. Choose either Default or Prominent.

Alternatively, you can open the Apple Watch application on your iPhone, tap My Watch, tap Sounds & Haptics, and then select Default or Prominent.

Digital Crown haptics can be activated or deactivated.

When scrolling on an Apple Watch using the Digital Crown, you can sense clicks. Follow these procedures to enable or disable these sounds:

1. On the Apple Watch, launch the Settings application.

2. Tap Sound & Haptics, then toggle Crown Haptics on or off.

You can also enable or disable system haptics.

Alternatively, open the Apple Watch app on your iPhone, tap My Watch, touch Sounds & Haptics, and then toggle Crown Haptics on or off.

Expect Taptic Time

When Apple Watch is in silent mode, it can display the time with a sequence of distinct taps on the wrist.

1. On the Apple Watch, launch the Settings application.
2. Tap Clock, then navigate to the bottom and tap Taptic Time.
3. Select either Digits, Terse, or Morse Code as the setting for Taptic Time.
- Digits: The Apple Watch performs a long tap every 10 hours, followed by a short tap every hour, a long tap every 10 minutes, and a short tap every minute thereafter.

- Short: The Apple Watch taps long every five hours, short every hour thereafter, and long every quarter hour.
- The Apple Watch displays the time in Morse code when each number is tapped.

Taptic Time can also be configured on the iPhone. Open the Apple Watch app on your iPhone, select My Watch, then navigate to Clock > Taptic Time to activate Taptic Time.

If Taptic Time is disabled, Apple Watch may be set to always display the time. To enable Taptic Time, navigate to Settings > Clock > Speak Time > Control with Silent Mode.

Chapter 5

See and respond to notifications on Apple Watch

Apps can send you notifications for meeting invitations, messages, pollution alerts, and Activity reminders, among other things. Your Apple Watch can display notifications as they arrive, but if you do not view one immediately, it will be stored so you can view it later.

When a message arrives, action must be taken.

1. Raise your wrist when you hear or sense an alert.

   Whether the screen is on or off influences the appearance of the notification.

- Active display: a small banner appears at the top of the screen.

- When the screen is not in use, a full-screen alert appears.

2. Touch the notification to view it.

3. Swipe down on a notification to dismiss it. Alternately, you can navigate to the bottom of the notification and then tap "Dismiss."

Examine the alerts you have not yet responded to.

If you do not respond to an alert immediately, it will be saved in the Notification Center. A red dot located at the top of your watch face indicates that you have unread messages. Follow the procedures below to view it:

1. Swipe down on the face of the watch to access the Notification Center. Touch and hold the top of the display, then swipe from other displays downwards.
   Note: You cannot access Notification Center from the Apple Watch's Home Screen. Instead, press the Digital Crown to navigate to the watch face or an application, and then press it again to access the Notification Center.
2. Swipe up or down or rotate the Digital Crown to browse through the list of notifications.
3. Touch the notification to view or reply.

To delete a notification without perusing it, swipe it to the left and tap the X icon. To delete all notifications, scroll to the top of the screen and select Clear All.

If you use group notifications, tap a group to open it, then press a notification.

Open the Settings app  on your Apple Watch, select Notifications, and then disable Notifications Indicator to prevent the red dot from displaying on the watch face.

Swipe down to view unread notifications.

Apple Watch notifications can be disabled.

Touch and hold the bottom of the screen, then swipe up to access the Control Center and tap 🔔.

You still receive a nudge when an alert arrives. Follow the methods below to eliminate noise and taps:

1. To access Control Center, tap and hold the bottom of the display, then swipe up.

2. Tap 🌙 or the Focus that is active.

3. Tap "Do not disturb," then select "On," "On for 1 hour," "On until tonight/tomorrow morning," or "On until I leave."

When you receive an alert on your Apple Watch, you can muffle it by placing your palm on the display for at least three seconds. A touch will indicate that the mute is activated. Make sure Cover to Mute is enabled. Open the Apple Watch Settings app, select Sounds & Haptics, and then toggle Cover to Mute.

Apple Watch settings for notifications are modifiable.

When you set up an Apple Watch, the default settings for app notifications are identical to those on your iPhone. But some applications allow you to customize how notifications appear.

Note: that you cannot use mirrored settings on a family member's Apple Watch that you manage.

You can select how applications send you notifications.

1. On your iPhone, launch the Apple Watch app.

2. Select My Watch, followed by Notifications.

3. Select the application (such as Messages), then select Custom, and then choose an option. Some options include:

- Allow Notifications: If you select this option, notifications will be sent to the Notification Center.

- Send to Notification Center: Notifications are sent directly to Notification Center without sounding or displaying on the Apple Watch.

- Notifications are disabled: the application does not send alerts.

4. grouping application alerts: Determine how the app's notifications are organized. Some options include:

- Off: Notifications are not compiled.

- Automatically, your Apple Watch creates distinct categories based on the app's data. News notifications, for instance, are organized according to the channels you follow, such as CNN, Washington Post, and People.

- By App: Notifications for a given application are grouped together.

Some applications allow you to select the types of notifications you wish to receive. You can choose to receive Calendar notifications only when certain events occur, such as when someone sends you an invitation or modifies a shared calendar. You can select which email accounts are permitted to send notifications via Mail.

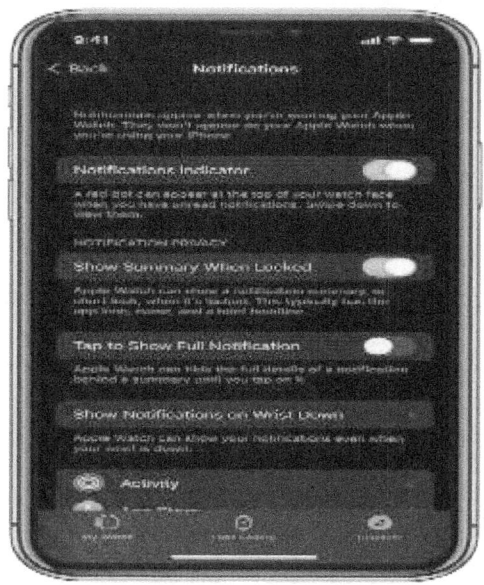

Apple Watch allows you to modify the configuration of notifications.

You can modify the settings for other alerts directly on your Apple Watch by swiping left and tapping on an alert. Some options include:

- **Mute for 1 hour or Today:** Notifications are routed directly to the Notification Center for the next hour or the remainder of the day. The Apple Watch will not produce a vibration or display the notification. Swipe left on an alert, touch, and then tap Unmute to view and hear these notifications again.

- **Add to Summary:** Notifications from the application will appear in the iPhone's Notifications Summary.
  Launch the iPhone's Settings app, tap Notifications, touch the app, and then tap Immediate Delivery. This will prompt the app to notify you immediately once more.

- **Disable Time Sensitive.** Even if you are using a Focus, which delays most notifications, time-sensitive alerts are always delivered immediately. Tap this option to prevent this app from sending you notifications immediately, even if they are time-sensitive.

- **Off:** The application no longer sends notifications. To re-enable app notifications, open the Apple Watch app on your iPhone, tap My Watch, tap Notifications, touch the app whose notifications you wish to modify, and then tap Allow Notifications.

Show notifications on the lock screen

You can customize how notifications appear on the lock screen of your smartwatch.

1. On your Apple Watch, launch the Settings application.
2. Select "Notifications."
3. Select one from the following:

*   Show Summary When Locked: If this option is enabled, your Apple Watch will display a summary of notifications when it is locked. The summary includes the app's name and icon as well as a brief headline.

*   Tap for the complete message: When you elevate your wrist to examine a notification, a brief summary appears. A few seconds later, you see the complete information. For example, when you receive a message, you view the sender's name and then the message itself. If this setting is enabled, the complete notification will not appear until you tap it.

- Display Notifications When Wrist Is Down: By default, the Apple Watch does not display notifications when the wrist is down. Enable this option to receive notifications even when your Apple Watch is not visible.

Apple Watch permits the change of Apple ID settings.

You can glance at and change the information about your Apple ID. You can alter your password, add a trusted phone number, and add and edit your contact information, among other options.

Alter your contact information

1. On your Apple Watch, launch the Settings application.
2. 2.Toggle [your user name].
3. Tap Name, Phone Numbers, and Email, and then perform one of the subsequent actions:

- Modify the name: Select your name, then select First, Middle, or Last.
- Examine, modify, and add contact information: Under "Reachable At," select a telephone number or email address. select the email address to delete, then select Remove Email Address.
- Include telephone and email addresses: Tap Add Email or Phone Number, select an email address or phone number to add, tap Next, input the information, then tap Done.
- To conceal your email address: Select Next.

- With this setting, apps can get in contact with you without getting your real email address. If you select this option, Apple will generate a unique, arbitrary email address for you. Any emails sent to this address by the application will be forwarded to the personal address you specify.
- Make your celebration exceptional: Tap Birthday, then enter an alternative date.
- Receive the Apple News newsletter, updates, and suggestions: Under "Subscriptions," you can activate "Announcements," "Recommendations," and "Apple News Newsletter."

Manage your Apple ID's password and security settings.

1. On your Apple Watch, launch the Settings application .
2. 2.Toggle [your user name].
3. Tap Password & Security, and then perform one of the subsequent actions:

- Modify the passphrase for your Apple ID: Tap Change Password, then follow the on-screen instructions.
- Modify the settings for "Sign in with Apple" on a website or app: Tap Apps Using Your Apple ID, followed by a selection. To halt the app from using your Apple ID, tap halt Using Apple ID. (The next time you use the app to sign in, you may be required to create a new account.)

- To edit or add a trusted phone number, tap your current trusted phone number, then press Remove Phone Number. If you have only one trusted number, you must add a new one before deleting the existing one.
- To sign in on another device or at iCloud.com, obtain a verification code by tapping Add a Trusted Phone Number. Click the Get Auth Code button.

Consider subscriptions and administer them

1. On your Apple Watch, launch the Settings application .
2. 2.Toggle [your user name].
3. touch Subscriptions, then touch a subscription to view details about it, such as its price and duration.
4. Tap Cancel Subscription to cancel your subscription.

Note: You must deactivate some iPhone subscriptions.

You can monitor and manage your devices.

1. On your Apple Watch, launch the Settings application .
2. 2.Toggle [your user name].
3. Scroll down and select a device to view its specifications.
4. If the device is unknown, select "Remove from Account."

Use Apple Watch shortcuts

Using the Apple Watch Shortcuts app, you can perform actions with a single swipe. You can rapidly find your way home, compile a list of the top 25 songs, and perform other tasks with iPhone shortcuts. Shortcuts can be executed via the Shortcuts app or applied as complications to your watch face.

Not all iPhone shortcuts are compatible with Apple Watch.

Create a shortcut.

1. On your Apple Watch, launch the Shortcuts application

    .

2. Tap a shortcut link.

Include a shortcut issue.

1. Touch and hold the watch face, then touch the Edit button.
2. Swipe to the left to access the "Complications" screen, then select one of the problems.

3. Scroll down until you see Shortcuts, then select one of them.

Apple Watch requires additional shortcuts.

1. On your iPhone, launch the Shortcuts application.

2. Tap ● ● ● the shortcut's upper right corner.

3. Touch ⓘ the shortcut screen and toggle Show on Apple Watch.

Apple Watch supports the configuration of handwashing reminders.

Apple Watch can notify and remind you to continue cleansing your hands for the recommended 20 seconds, as recommended by global health organizations. If you haven't washed your hands in a few minutes after returning home, your Apple Watch can remind you to do so.

Configure hand cleaning on the Apple Watch.

1. On your Apple Watch, launch the Settings application.
2. Select Handwashing, then activate Handwashing Timer.

When Apple Watch detects that you've begun washing your hands, it begins a 20-second timer. If you pause while washing for less than 20 seconds, you should continue.

Remind yourself to cleanse your hands.

Apple Watch can remind you to cleanse your hands when you return home.

1. On your Apple Watch, launch the Settings application.
2. Select Handwashing, then activate Handwashing Reminders.

You can also set handwashing reminders for family members on an Apple Watch. Open the Settings app on the managed Apple Watch, select Handwashing, toggle the Handwashing Timer and Handwashing Reminders settings.

Set your home address in the My Card section of the iPhone's Contacts app to receive reminders to cleanse your hands.

Open the Health app on your iPhone, navigate to Browse > Other Data, and then select Handwashing to view a report of the average amount of time you spend washing your hands.

Apple Watch connects to a Wi-Fi network.

By connecting your Apple Watch to a Wi-Fi network, you can use a number of its features without your iPhone.

Select a wireless network to use.

1. To access Control Center, tap and hold the bottom of the display, then swipe up.

2. Touch and hold, then select the name of a Wi-Fi network 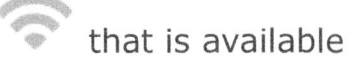 that is available.

   Apple Watch is compatible with 2.4GHz 802.11b/g/n Wi-Fi networks.

3. If you need a network password, you can do one of the following:

- Enter the password using the Apple Watch's keyboard (not available in all languages; only on Apple Watch Series 7 and Apple Watch Series 8).

- Use your finger to write the characters of the password on the screen. Use the Digital Crown to select whether or not to use capital letters.

- Tap 🔑 followed by selecting a password from the list.

- Use the iPhone's keyboard to enter the password.

4. Tap Join.

Apple Watch can be configured to use a private network address.

On every Wi-Fi network it joins, your Apple Watch employs a unique private network address called a media access control (MAC) address to protect your privacy. Stop using a private address for a network if it cannot use one (for example, to give parents control or to indicate that your Apple Watch is permitted to join).

1. To access Control Center, tap and hold the bottom of the display, then swipe up.

2. Touch and hold 📶 the name of the network you just joined, then tap it.

3. Prevent Private Address from functioning.

Leaving Private Address enabled on all networks that support it will increase your privacy. Utilizing a private address on your Apple Watch makes it more difficult to track it across various Wi-Fi networks.

Regardless of a network

1. To access Control Center, tap and hold the bottom of the display, then swipe up.

2. Touch and hold 📶 the name of the network you just joined, then tap it.

3. Tap "Forget This Network."

If you wish to use this network again in the future, you will need to re-enter its password.

Chapter 6

Connect Apple Watch to Bluetooth headphones or speakers

You can stream music from your Apple Watch to Bluetooth headphones or speakers even when your iPhone is not nearby.

If you set up your AirPods with your iPhone, you can use them with your Apple Watch simply by tapping the play button.

It is possible to connect Bluetooth headphones and speakers.

The majority of audio on your Apple Watch requires Bluetooth headphones or speakers (Siri, phone calls, voicemail, and voice memos all play through the Apple Watch's speaker). Follow the included instructions to place the headphones or speakers into discovery mode. When the Bluetooth device is prepared, follow these steps:

1. Launch the Apple Watch Settings application , then select Bluetooth.
2. When a device appears, tap it.

You can also access Bluetooth settings by tapping on the play screens of the Audiobooks, Music, Now Playing, and Podcasts applications.

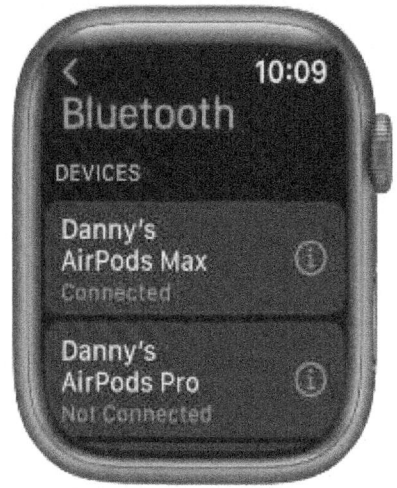 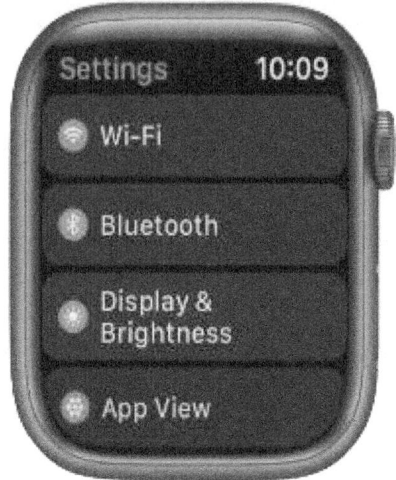

Choose a display mode

1. To access Control Center, contact and hold the bottom of the screen, then swipe upwards.

2. Tap the device you wish to use, then select it.

Examine the volume of your headphones.

1. To access Control Center, contact and hold the bottom of the screen, then swipe upwards.

2. While wearing headphones, you must tap .

A meter indicates the current volume level of headphones.

Reduce the noise

Apple Watch allows you to set a decibel limit for how noisy your headphones can be.

1. Launch the Settings program on your Apple Watch.
2. Go to Sounds & Haptics > Headphone Safety, and then tap Reduce Loud Sounds.

3. Activate Reduce Loud Sounds and set a level.

Listen to alerts with headphones at maximum volume

If you listen to loud music on your headphones for an extended period of time that could damage your hearing, Apple Watch sends you a headphone alert and automatically lowers the volume to safeguard your hearing.

Launch the Health app on your iPhone, tap Browse, tap Hearing, tap Headphone Notifications, and then select a notification for more information.

Apple Watch is able to bypass duties.

Handoff enables you to transition between devices without having to pause your current activity. For example, you could use the Mail app on your Apple Watch to reply to an email, but you may want to transition to your iPhone so that you can use the onscreen keyboard to respond. You can use Handoff if you configure your Apple Watch. You are unable to use Handoff if you set up an Apple Watch for a family member. Perform these steps to use Handoff.

1. Activate your iPhone.
2. To access the App Switcher on an iPhone equipped with Face ID, swipe up from the bottom edge and pause.
3. To access the identical item on your iPhone, tap the button at the bottom of the display.

If you do not see an icon in App Switcher, navigate to Settings > General > AirPlay & Handoff on your iPhone and ensure that Handoff is enabled.

The transfer has begun. To disable it, open the Apple Watch app on your iPhone, tap My Watch, touch General, and then toggle off the Enable Handoff option.

Handoff is compatible with the subsequent applications: Activity, Alarm, Calendar, Home, Mail, Maps, Messages, Music, News, Phone, Podcasts, Reminders, Settings, Siri, Stocks, Stopwatch, Timers, Wallet, Weather, and World Clock. For Handoff to function, you must have already connected your Apple Watch with your iPhone.

Apple Watch is capable of unlocking a Mac.

If your Mac was manufactured after mid-2013 and runs macOS 10.13 or later, you can unlock it with your Apple Watch as soon as it powers up. On both your Mac and your Apple Watch, you need to be enrolled in to iCloud with the same Apple ID.

To determine the model year of your Mac, click the Apple menu in the upper left corner of the display and then click About This Mac. The year your Mac was manufactured is displayed alongside the model, such as "MacBook Pro (15-inch, 2018"

Turn on Automatic Locking

1. Verify the following configurations on your devices:
- Your Mac has both Wi-Fi and Bluetooth enabled.
- Your Mac and Apple Watch are both signed in to iCloud using the same Apple ID and two-factor authentication is enabled for your Apple ID.
- Your Apple Watch possesses a passcode.

2. From the menu bar, select Apple > System Preferences.

3. Select Security & Privacy followed by General.

4. Choose "Use your Apple Watch to unlock apps and your Mac."

Choose which Apple Watch you want to use to access your Mac and other devices if you possess more of them.

If you haven't activated two-factor authentication for your Apple ID yet, follow the on-screen instructions and then try again.

Launch Mac OS

When you are donning a watch, you do not need to enter your password to wake up your Mac.

Ensure that your Apple Watch is on your wrist and unlocked, and that you are close to your Mac.

Apple Watch can unlock your iPhone.

To enable Apple Watch to unlock your iPhone when Siri asks it to or when Face ID cannot due to an obstruction, perform the steps below:

1. Enter your passcode after accessing Settings > Face ID & Passcode on your iPhone.
2. Scroll until you see "Unlock with Apple Watch," then adjust your watch's settings.
   Ensure that each of your watches is set to the correct time if you own multiple.
3. Make sure you're wearing your Apple Watch, activate your iPhone, and then glance at its screen to unlock it.

Apple Watch vibrates your wrist to notify you when your iPhone is accessible.

Note: Your Apple Watch must have a passcode, be unlocked and on your wrist, and be in close proximity to your iPhone for it to activate.

Apple Watch can be used without an iPhone.

Apple Watch can function independently of an iPhone.

If you have an Apple Watch with cellular and a cellular plan that is activated, you can remain connected even when you are away from your iPhone. Even if you are away from your iPhone and not connected to Wi-Fi, you are still able to perform certain tasks with all other Apple Watch models.

- Use Apple Watch to listen to music;
- use Apple Watch to listen to podcasts
- use Apple Watch to listen to audiobooks
- allow recording and playback of voice memos on Apple Watch;
- utilize your transit card and student ID;
- Locate individuals, objects, and tools.
- Utilize the timepiece, world clock, alarms, schedules, and stopwatch.
- Display images taken from synced photo albums.
- Make purchases in stores using Apple Pay.
- Consult your Apple Watch for your calendar information.
- Maintain a log of your exercise routine.
- Check your heart rate, modify the way you sleep, measure your blood oxygen levels, keep note of your menstrual cycles, and take a few deep breaths.
- Determine the ambient decibel level and the headphone volume.

Apple Watch has a built-in GPS, so you can get more accurate distance and pace data when working out outdoors without your iPhone. Apple Watch also includes a barometric altimeter so that elevation gain or loss can be measured with greater precision. The altimeter on the Apple Watch SE, Apple Watch Series 6, and later models is more precise and displays your current elevation in real-time.

If your Apple Watch is connected to Wi-Fi, you can send and receive data wirelessly.

Even if your iPhone is off, you can still do the following with your Apple Watch when it is connected to a Wi-Fi network:

- Download programs from the App Store
- Send messages using the Apple Watch
- If Wi-Fi calling is enabled or if you want to make a FaceTime audio call and are near a Wi-Fi network, you can make calls on your Apple Watch.
- The Walkie-Talkie feature is also available.
- You can stream music, podcasts, and audiobooks to your Apple Watch.
- The Apple Watch can accommodate music.
- The weather can be checked.
- Your securities can be followed.
- Control your home using your Apple Watch.
- Utilize Wi-Fi-capable third-party applications.

The Apple Watch connects to your iPhone via Bluetooth® wireless technology and utilizes your iPhone for a number of wireless functions. Your Apple Watch can set up Wi-Fi networks independently and connect to networks you've created or joined with your iPhone.

Apple Watch supports cellular networks.

With an Apple Watch with cellular and a cellular connection to the same carrier as your iPhone, you can make calls, reply to messages, use Walkie-Talkie, stream music and podcasts, receive notifications, and more without your iPhone or a Wi-Fi connection.

Please be aware that cell phone service is not available everywhere or from every service provider.

Apple Watch is compatible with cellular phone plans.

To enable cellular service on your Apple Watch, follow the instructions provided during initial setup. Follow these steps to later activate service:

1. Start the Apple Watch app on your iPhone.
2. Select Cellular after selecting My Watch.

Turn on or off your mobile device.

Your cellular-enabled Apple Watch utilizes the optimal network connection available. This could be your iPhone if it is nearby, a Wi-Fi network to which you have already connected your iPhone, or a cellular connection. If you wish to conserve battery power, you can disable cellular. Do only the following:

1. To access Control Center, contact and hold the bottom of the screen, then swipe upwards.

2. Tap $^{((\cdot))}$ and toggle Cellular on and off.

When your Apple Watch is connected to a cellular network and your iPhone is not nearby, the Cellular button turns orange.

Note: prolonging the use of cellular depletes the battery more. Additionally, some applications may be unable to be updated if they cannot communicate with your iPhone.

Check the cell signal strength.

Attempt one of the following when connected to a cellular network:

- Employ the Explorer display, which indicates the strength of your cellular signal with green specks. Four dots establish a good connection. One dot is inferior.
- Launch Control Panel. Green bands at the top indicate the cellular connection.
- Integrate the Cellular feature into the watch face.

Check mobile data usage

1. Start the Settings program on your Apple Watch.
2. Tap Cellular, and then navigate down to view the amount of data used during this period.

Set up and view your Medical ID on Apple Watch

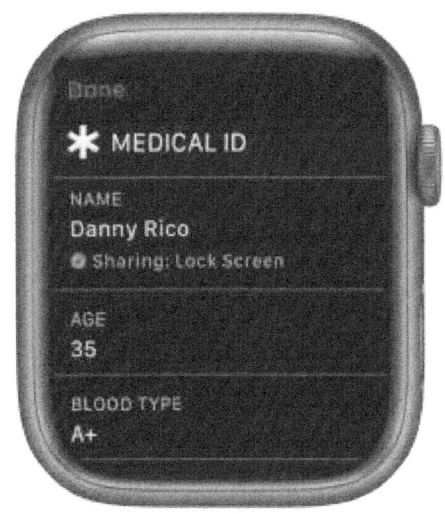

A Medical ID reveals your allergies and medical conditions, which may be crucial in an emergency. When you set up your Medical ID in the Health app on your iPhone, the information is synced with your Apple Watch. If you share your Medical ID, when you call or text 911 or use Emergency SOS, your Apple Watch can send emergency services your medical information (U.S. and Canada only).

Your Medical ID can be displayed on your Apple Watch, allowing those who assist you in an emergency to view it.

Follow these instructions to display your Medical ID on your Apple Watch:

1. Until the sliders appear, press and hold the side button.
2. Move the slider to the right for Medical ID.
3. Tap Done once you're finished.

Apple Watch users can also access SOS > Medical ID via the Settings app .

Apple Watch enables communication with emergency services.

Use your Apple Watch to swiftly summon assistance when you're in trouble.

If you need aid, dial 911.

Select one of these:

- Hold down the side button until the sliders appear, then drag the Emergency Call slider to the right.

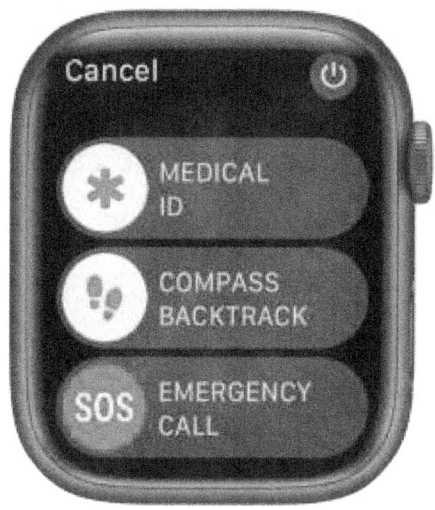

  Your Apple Watch contacts the local emergency services, including 911. (In some locations, you may be required to enter a number on the keypad in order to end the contact.)

- Press and hold the side button until your Apple Watch emits an alert tone and begins a countdown. Apple Watch contacts the police or fire department when the timer expires. Even if your Apple Watch is in silent mode, it will continue to emit the alert sound. If you're in a dire situation and don't want to make noise, you can use the Emergency summon slider to summon for assistance without a countdown.

Turn off Automatic Dialing if you do not want your Apple Watch to begin an emergency countdown when you press and hold the side button. Open your Apple Watch's Settings app , tap SOS, tap Hold Side Button, and then turn off Hold Side Button. (Or, on your iPhone, open the Apple Watch app, tap "My Watch," touch "Emergency SOS," and then disable "Hold Side Button to Dial.") With the Emergency Call slider, you can still make an emergency call.

- Say to Siri, "Hey, dial 911"

- On your Apple Watch, launch the Messages app , tap New Message, tap Add Contact, touch the number pad, and then type 911. Tap "Create Message," enter your message, and then tap "Send."

If Fall Detection is enabled and you have not moved for about a minute after Apple Watch detects a forceful fall, it will attempt to automatically dial 911.

If your Apple Watch detects a severe automobile accident, it will display an alert and, after 20 seconds, it will dial an emergency number.

In many locations where cellular service is accessible, an Apple Watch Series 5 (GPS + Cellular), Apple Watch SE (GPS + Cellular), Apple Watch Series 6 (GPS + Cellular), Apple Watch Series 7 (GPS + Cellular), or Apple Watch Series 8 can be used to initiate an emergency call. Some cellular networks may not accept an emergency call from your Apple Watch Series 5, Apple Watch SE, Apple Watch Series 6, Apple Watch Series 7 (GPS + Cellular), or Apple Watch Series 8 if it isn't activated, compatible with or set up to work on a certain cellular network, or configured for cellular service.

Additionally, you may add emergency contacts. The Apple Watch sends a text message to your emergency contacts when an emergency call terminates, unless you cancel. Your Apple Watch transmits your current location, and for a period of time after activating SOS mode, if your location changes, your emergency contacts will receive a notification.

When you initiate an Emergency SOS call while you're abroad, your Apple Watch connects to local emergency services, but it does not transmit your location or a message to your emergency contacts. In some locations, you can make international emergency contacts even if you haven't activated cell service on your watch.

Cancel an emergency call

touch and then touch End Call to terminate an emergency call made in error.

Change your emergency mailing address

In the event that emergency services cannot locate you, they will travel to the address you provided.

1. Start the Settings program on your iPhone.

2. Go to Phone > Wi-Fi Calling, select Update Emergency Address, and then type in your emergency address.

Manage fall detection on the Apple Watch

If you have Fall Detection enabled, Apple Watch can connect you to emergency services and send a message to your emergency contacts in the event of a severe fall. If you take a hard fall and do not move for about a minute, Apple Watch will tap your wrist, sound an alarm, and attempt to contact the police.

If you are at least 55 years old when you set up your Apple Watch or add it to the Health app on your iPhone, Fall Detection will be automatically enabled. If you are between the ages of 18 and 55, you can manually enable Fall Detection by following these steps:

1. Launch the Settings program on your Apple Watch.

2. Turn on Fall Detection by navigating to SOS > Fall Detection.

Additionally, you can use your iPhone to launch the Apple Watch app, tap My Watch, press Emergency SOS, and then enable Fall Detection.

Note: If you disable wrist detection, Apple Watch will not automatically attempt to call 911 after a heavy impact fall, even if you've set it to do so.

3. Choose "Always on" if you want Fall Detection to be on all the time, or "Only during workouts" if you only want it on when you're working out.

Fall Detection is automatically enabled during exercises for users between the ages of 18 and 55 who have set up a new Apple Watch with watchOS 8.1 or later. If you convert your Apple Watch from an earlier version of watchOS, you must activate the feature to only detect hard falls during workouts.

Handle Apple Watch Crash Detection

If your Apple Watch Series 8 or Apple Watch SE (2nd Generation) detects a severe car accident, it can assist you in contacting emergency services and notifying emergency contacts.

If the Apple Watch detects a severe car accident, it will automatically dial 911 after 20 seconds if you do not intervene. If you do not respond, it will play an audio message informing emergency service that you were involved in a severe car accident and providing them with your latitude and longitude coordinates as well as an approximate search radius.

Note that if a severe car accident is detected, Crash Detection will not halt any other emergency calls that have already been placed.

Crashes are detected by default.

It can be disabled. After a severe car accident, take the following steps to disable Apple's alerts and automatic emergency calls:

1. Launch the Settings program on your Apple Watch.
2. Turn it off by going to SOS > Crash Detection > Call After Severe Crash in the menu.

Chapter 7

Use Siri on Apple Watch

Effective Siri commands

You can use Siri on your Apple Watch to do things and get answers. Siri can, for instance, translate what you say into another language, identify a song and provide an instant Shazam result, or, in response to a general query, display the top few search results along with a brief excerpt from each page. Tap Open Page on Apple Watch to view the page. Consider using Siri to accomplish tasks that normally require several steps.

Siri is not available in every location or language.

Siri: Use phrases such as:

- "What does "How are you?" mean in Chinese?"
  Begin a 30-minute outdoor run. Inform Kathleen that I am nearly finished.
- "Open the Sleep app"
- "What's the name of this song?"
- "Why do rainbows happen?"
- "What's going on?"
- "What sorts of questions can I ask?"

How to speak with Siri

Use any of the following to pose a question to Siri:

- Raise your wrist and speak into the Apple Watch microphone.

  To disable Raise to Speak, open the Settings app on your Apple Watch, select Siri, and then turn off Raise to Speak.

- Say "Hey Siri" followed by your request.

  To disable "Hey Siri," launch the Settings app on your Apple Watch, select Siri, and then toggle off Listen for "Hey Siri."

- Tap the Siri icon on the watch's face.

Press and maintain the Digital Crown until the "Listening" indicator light illuminates. Then, state your intentions.

Open the Settings app on your Apple Watch, select Siri, and then turn off Press Digital Crown to disable Press Digital Crown.

After Siri has been activated, you can release your forearm. When a user responds, you will experience a tap.

Siri can answer a query or continue a conversation if you hold down the Digital Crown and speak to her.

Siri, just as it does on iOS, macOS, and macOS, can provide direction. Additionally, you can connect a Bluetooth earpiece or speakers to Apple Watch to hear Siri's responses through them.

Apple Watch must be connected to the internet for Siri to function. There could be mobile phone fees.

Choose how Siri will respond.

Siri on your Apple Watch can speak responses. Launch the Settings app on your Apple Watch, tap Siri, touch Siri Responses, and then select from the options below:

- Siri speaks responses even when the Apple Watch is in muted mode.
- When your Apple Watch is in inactive mode, Siri will not respond.
- Open the Settings app on your Apple Watch, tap Siri, then tap Language or Siri Voice to alter Siri's language or voice.

Only with Headphones: Siri will only respond when your Apple Watch is connected to Bluetooth headphones. When you select Siri Voice, you can choose from a variety of voices.

Not all languages offer the ability to alter Siri Voice.

Show captions and written versions of your Siri commands

Your Apple Watch can display captions and transcriptions of your conversations with Siri and Siri's responses. To toggle Always Show Siri Captions and Always Show Speech, open the Settings app on your Apple Watch and select Siri.

When Siri is instructed to halt time, it does so.

If you have difficulty speaking, you can type Siri commands or request that Siri wait longer for you to complete speaking.

1. On your Apple Watch, launch the Settings application.
2. Navigate to Accessibility > Siri and activate Type to Siri.
3. Tap Longer or Longest under Siri Pause Time if you want Siri to wait for you to conclude speaking for a longer period of time.

Remove Siri's history.

When you use Siri or dictation, your queries are stored for six months on Apple's servers so Siri can become more adept at answering your questions. Not your Apple ID or email address, but a random number is linked to your requests. You can remove these interactions from the server at any time.

1. On your Apple Watch, launch the Settings application.
2. Tap Siri, then tap Siri History, followed by Delete Siri History.

Apple Watch supports AirPods and Beats headphones for listening to and responding to notifications.

When using AirPods or Beats headphones that are compatible with Siri, she can read out notifications from a number of applications without requiring you to unlock your iPhone. Siri will not speak unless you ask her to, and she will listen after reading you a message so that you can respond without uttering "Hey Siri."

Turn on "Announce Notifications."

1. Depending on the sort of headphones you own, insert or place them on your ears.
2. Use Apple Watch to join the two devices.
3. Open the Apple Watch's Settings application.
4. Navigate to Siri > Announce Notifications and toggle Announce Notifications on.

Additionally, you can launch the Settings application on your iPhone, navigate to Notifications > Announce Notifications, and then enable Announce Notifications.

Select which applications will send you notifications.

You can choose which applications can send you notifications.

1. Depending on the sort of headphones you own, insert or place them on your ears.
2. 2.launch the Apple Watch's Settings application.

3. Navigate to Siri > Announce Notifications, scroll down, and then select the desired app notifications.

Disable Announce Notifications for the time being.

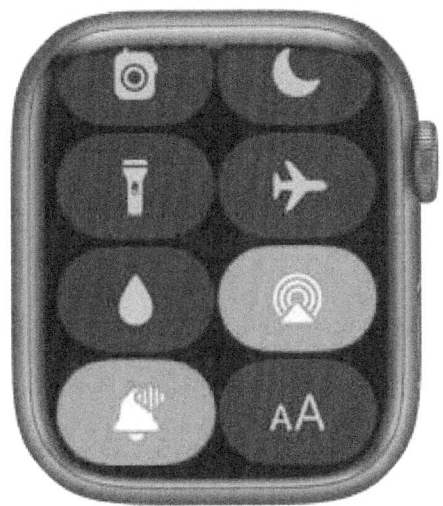

1. To access Control Center, tap and hold the bottom of the display, then swipe up.

2. Tap   .

To activate it, touch it again.

When you remove your AirPods, the Announce Notifications button becomes inactive.

React to a message

Respond with something like, "That's fantastic news."

Siri repeats what you said and then requests affirmation before delivering your reply. Open the Settings app on your Apple Watch, navigate to Siri > Announce Notifications, scroll to the bottom, and enable Reply without Confirmation.

Siri should not recite a message aloud.

It is possible for any of the following to occur:

- Inform the individual to "Stop" or "Cancel."
- Maintain pressure on the Digital Crown (AirPods Max).
  Note: You can adjust the intensity of a notification while you are listening to it by rotating the Digital Crown.
- Press one of the Force Sensor buttons (AirPods Pro or AirPods 3rd generation).
- Double-tap one of your AirPods (2nd generation).
- Remove one of your AirPods (AirPods Pro, AirPods 2nd generation, or AirPods 3rd generation).

If you did not enable Announce Notifications when you set up your AirPods, open the Settings app on your Apple Watch, navigate to Siri, and then Announce Notifications, and enable Announce Notifications.

Siri on Apple Watch allows you to announce incoming contacts.

With Announce Calls, Siri notifies you of incoming phone calls and FaceTime calls, and you can use your voice to accept or decline the call. Announce Calls is also compatible with third-party applications.

1. Launch the Settings app on your Apple Watch.
2. Tap Siri, and then enable Announce Calls.

3. When a call arrives, you are informed of who it's from and asked if you wish to accept it. If you wish to accept the contact, reply "yes." If you do not agree, say "no."

Explore the Face Gallery on Apple Watch

Face Gallery is the simplest method to view all of the watch faces in the Apple Watch app. When you discover one you like, you can modify it, add complications, and save it directly from the gallery.

Face Gallery is now accessible.

Open the Apple Watch app on your iPhone, then select Face Gallery.

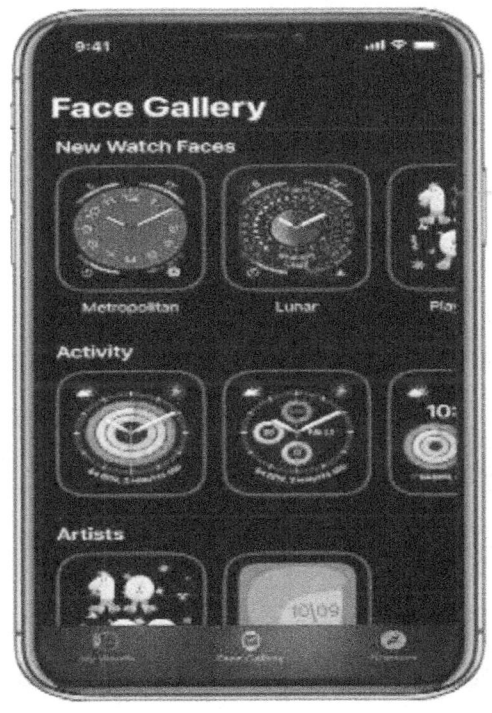

Tap a face to customize it and add it to your collection.

Remove portions of a visage.

touch a face from the Face Gallery, then touch a characteristic such as color or style.

As you experiment with various options, the face at the top of the screen will alter to ensure that the design is flawless.

Create changes to the Face Gallery.

1. Select a face from the Face Gallery, and then select a complication position, such as Top Left, Top Right, or Bottom.
2. Swipe to see what complications are available for that position, then select the one you want.
1. 3.Scroll to the top of the list and tap Off if you determine you do not want a complication in that location.

Add a face

1. After modifying a visage in the visage Gallery, tap Add.
2. Swipe left across the face of your Apple Watch until the new face appears.

Swap out the watch's face.

You're able to customize the appearance and functionality of the face of your Apple Watch. Choose a design, modify its colors and details, and add it to your collection. You can alternate clock faces at any time to view the correct time or to vary things.

The Face Gallery in the Apple Watch app is the easiest method to see all of the watch faces, customize one, and add it to your collection. However, if you do not have your iPhone with you, you can alter the face of the watch directly on the watch.

Replace your watch's face.

- Drag your finger from one side of the watch face to the opposite side to view the other faces in your collection.

- Touch and hold a watch face, then swipe and touch the desired face.

Swipe left or right to see other watch faces.

Simple

Add features to your watch face.

Add additional features to the watch face.

Some watch designs can be customized with additional features. These features are referred to as "complications," and they allow you to rapidly check the stock market, the weather, and information from other installed apps.

1. Touch and hold the display while the watch face is active, and then select Edit.

2. Swipe to the left until the end is reached.

   If a visage has issues, they will be displayed on the final screen.

3. Tap a complication to select it, then rotate the Digital Crown to select another one, such as Activity or Heart Rate.

4. When finished, press the Digital Crown to save your adjustments, and then tap the face to switch to it.

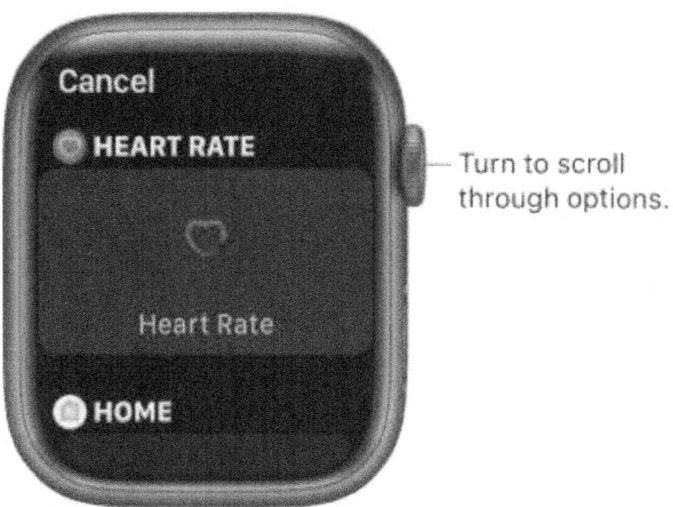

Some of the App Store's offerings may also be difficult to use.

Add a watch face to your existing watch.

You are able to create your own collection of custom features, including multiple variations of the same design.

1. Touch and hold the screen that displays the current watch face.

2. Swipe left until you reach the end, then tap the plus sign (+).

3. Turn the Digital Crown to browse the watch faces, then press the Add button.

In watchOS, select a collection such as "New" to view a specific category of watch faces.

You can alter the watch face after it has been added.

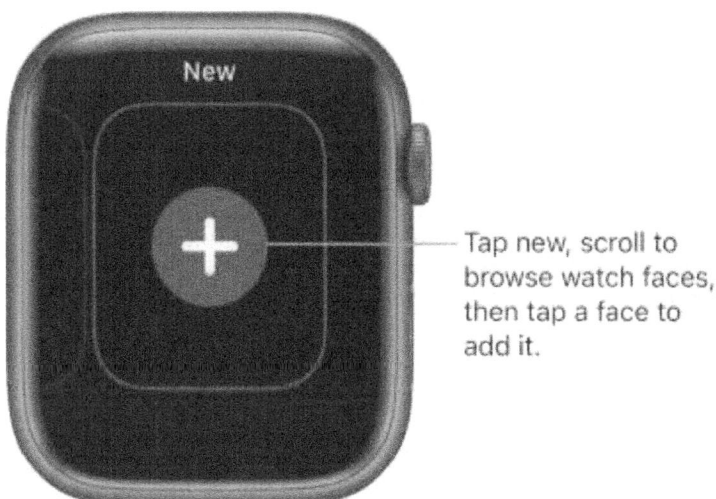

Tap new, scroll to browse watch faces, then tap a face to add it.

Consider your items.

You can see the faces of all your watches at a glimpse.

1. On your iPhone, launch the Apple Watch application.
2. Select My Watch and then use the arrows below My Faces to navigate your collection.

To alter the order of your collection, select Edit and then drag a watch face up or down.

Remove one of the identities you possess.

1. Touch and hold the screen that displays the current watch face.
2. Swipe to the unwanted visage, then swipe up and select Remove.

Alternatively, open the Apple Watch app on your iPhone, press My Watch, and then tap Edit under My Faces. select  the faces that you wish to remove, and then select Remove.

The watch face can be added at any time in the future.

Swipe up to delete a watch face, then tap Remove.

Move the clock forward

1. On your Apple Watch, launch the Settings application.
2. Press "Clock."
3. Tap +0 min, then rotate the Digital Crown to advance the timepiece by up to 59 minutes.

This setting only modifies the watch's face time. It does not alter alarm times, notification times, or other times (such as the World Clock).

Share watch faces for Apple Watch

Friends are able to exchange watch skins. Both watchOS-integrated complications and third-party complications can be used on shared faces.

Note: The recipient must also have an Apple Watch with watchOS 7 or a later version.

Share an analog timepiece face

1. Display the desired watch face on your Apple Watch.

2. Touch and hold the screen, then touch ⬆️.

3. Tap the name of the watch face. If you do not wish to disclose any complications, tap "Don't include."

4. Select a recipient, then select Messages or Mail.

    You can add a contact, subject (Mail), and message when you select Messages or Mail.

5. Select Send.

Open the Apple Watch app, select a watch face from collection or Face Gallery, select ⬆️, and then select share option.

Obtain a dial for a timepiece.

You can obtain shared watch faces in Messages, Mail, or by clicking a link online.

1. Launch a shared watch face-containing text, email, or link.
2. select the shared watch face, then select Add.

If a third-party app provides you with a watch face that includes a complication, select the app's price or Get to download it from the App Store. Alternatively, you can select Continue Without This App to view the watch face without the third-party complication.

Chapter 8

All about Apple Fitness+

When you sign up for Apple Fitness+, you gain access to a variety of activities, including HIIT, Yoga, Core, Cycling, Strength, Treadmill (running and walking), and Dance, among others. During a workout, your Apple Watch transmits your heart rate and calories expended to your iPhone, iPad, or Apple TV.

You can also participate in guided meditations designed to help you feel better in every way.

Apple Fitness+ requires an Apple Watch Series 3 or later with watchOS 7.2 or later, along with an iPhone 6s or later with iOS 14.3 or later, an iPad with iPadOS 14.3 or later, or an Apple TV 4K or Apple TV HD with tvOS 14.3 or later.

Apple Fitness+ requires an iPhone 8 or later with iOS 16, an iPad with iPadOS 16, an Apple TV 4K or Apple TV HD with tvOS 16, and an Apple Watch Series 4 or later with watchOS 9 to access the most recent features.

Please be aware that Apple Fitness+ is not accessible everywhere.

Select a form of exercise.

When it's time to exercise, you have a variety of options. You can view information about each workout, such as its playlist and music style, whether it has closed captions, and what apparatus you may need to perform the workout, such as dumbbells or a mat (most workouts do not require equipment). In addition, you can preview the workout before you begin.

Locate a coach.

Each Apple Fitness+ trainer has his or her own distinct personality, musical preferences, and training style. In the Fitness app, you can view a summary of each trainer's workouts and read about their background.

Check your totals

You can monitor your iPhone, iPad, or Apple TV during your workout to see how far you've progressed in each of your rings and how many calories you've burned.

With watchOS 9, Fitness+ regimens incorporate both trainer coaching and on-screen instructions to maximize their effectiveness. On-screen metrics include Intensity for HIIT, Cycling, Rowing, and Treadmill, Strokes per Minute (SPM) for Rowing, Revolutions per Minute (RPM) for Cycling, and Incline for Treadmill walkers and runners.

In cycling, HIIT, rowing, and treadmill regimens, the Burn Bar compares your metrics to those of individuals who have previously completed the workout. The more calories you expend, the higher you are on the expend Bar. Your Burn Bar position is preserved alongside your other workout metrics in the workout summary.

Enroll in Apple Fitness+.

You can consolidate your Apple Fitness+ subscription with other Apple services if you enroll in Apple One Premier.

Apple Fitness+ and Apple One Premier are not accessible in all countries and regions.

Download the app for fitness

Apple Fitness+ requires the Fitness application to be installed on your iPhone, iPad, or Apple TV. If you do not already have it, you can obtain the Fitness app from the App Store.

Enroll in Apple Fitness+.

1. Open the Fitness app on your iPhone, iPad, or Apple TV. Tap the Fitness+ icon if you are using an iPhone.
2. Follow the instructions on-screen to sign in with your Apple ID and validate your subscription after clicking the "Free Trial" button.

Cancel your subscription to Apple Fitness Plus

1. Choose among these:

- Launch the Fitness app on an iPhone or iPad, and if using an iPhone, select Summary. Tap your profile picture, then [account name], and finally Apple Fitness+.
- Launch the Settings app on Apple TV, navigate to Users and Accounts > [account name] > Subscriptions, and select Apple Fitness+.

2. Follow the instructions displayed on-screen to modify or terminate your subscription.

Family Sharing enables you to share your Apple Fitness+ subscription with your family.

Family Sharing enables you to share your Apple Fitness+ or Apple One Premier subscription with as many as five family members. Apple Fitness+ requires nothing from your family group participants. As long as they have an Apple Watch Series 3 or later, Apple Fitness+ will be accessible the first time they launch the Fitness app following the activation of your subscription, so long as they have an Apple Watch Series 3 or later. If an Apple Watch was set up by a family member and the individual does not own an iPhone, they can still use Apple Fitness+ with an Apple TV or an iPad.

You can remove a Family Sharing group member to cease sharing your Apple Fitness+ subscription with the group.

Apple Fitness+ is compatible with Apple TV.

If you're running tvOS 14.3 or later, your Apple Watch synchronizes with the Fitness app on your Apple TV 4K or Apple TV HD.

Connect your Apple Watch and Apple TV.

Apple Fitness+ requires that you connect your Apple Watch to your Apple TV.

1. On Apple TV, launch the Fitness app.
2. Select your name, or "Other" if it is not listed.
   If no user is currently logged into your Apple TV, you may need to select Sign In in the Fitness app first.
3. Connect your Apple Watch by pressing the Connect button.
   Note: Before tapping Connect, you may need to launch the Workout app on your Apple Watch.
4. Tap Continue if prompted, and then enter the code from your Apple TV using your Apple Watch.

Apple TV requires watchOS 7.2 or later, an unlocked Apple Watch, and Bluetooth to begin an exercise.

Select who is going to gym.

If Family Sharing is enabled, the Fitness application on Apple TV makes it simple to alternate between family members. Apple Fitness+ subscribers who are not part of your Family Sharing group can also utilize your Apple TV to exercise.

1. Launch the Fitness application on your Apple TV.
2. Select your name, or "Other" if it is not listed.

   If no one is currently signed in to your Apple TV, you may need to navigate to the Fitness app and select Sign In before continuing.

3. To switch to a different family member or guest, select the account icon in the upper left corner of the Fitness app, followed by Sign out.

Explore the exercises and meditations available on Apple Fitness+.

Apple Fitness+ can assist you in discovering the optimal fitness, meditation, or routine. You can search for individual workouts or Meditations, launch a program with multiple episodes, sort and filter workouts of a specific category, or select a workout based on your activity level. All other forms of workouts begin after ten minutes, whereas Mindful Cooldown workouts begin after only five. Each week, new exercises are added. One can meditate for five, ten, or twenty minutes.

You can view exercises and receive advice

Apple Fitness+ provides workout suggestions based on what you do with the Workout app on your Apple Watch and your preferred applications that are compatible with the Health app. Apple Fitness+ will also recommend new trainers and workouts to supplement your regimen.

1. Open the Fitness app on your iPhone, iPad, or Apple TV. Tap the Fitness+ icon if you are using an iPhone.
2. Consider exercises and coaches:

- Search by category of workout: Use the left and right arrow keys to navigate through the various types of workouts displayed at the top of the screen.

- Time to Walk and Time to Run: Select audio workouts to play on your Apple Watch (exclusively for iPhone).

Tap "Add" to add a "Time to Walk" or "Time to Run" episode to the

Apple Athlete. Open the Workout app on your Apple Watch, tap

Audio Workouts, scroll down, tap Library, then touch the episode. To view additional episodes, scroll down, select "Time to Walk" or "Time to Run," and then rotate the Digital Crown.

With iOS 16, it is also possible to listen to episodes of Time to Walk and Time to Run on the iPhone.

- To view the featured workouts, navigate to sections such as "New Workouts," "New Meditations," "Workouts for Beginners," "Popular," "Simple and Quick," and "Workouts for Advanced Users."
- Browse by trainer: Scroll down to the row of trainers, then move to the left or right and select a trainer to view their workouts and filter workouts by type, duration, and music genre.
- Tap Show All to view a list of all educators on an iPhone or iPad.
- Keep Doing What You're Doing: Browse workouts with trainers and workout categories you frequently use with your Apple Watch or other fitness apps that are compatible with the Health app.
- Try something different: Investigate regimens that are similar to the ones you already do, but that have different trainers and suggested workout types to prevent your routine from becoming monotonous.
- My Library: Workouts added to My Library from the detail or summary screens of a workout. This capability is exclusive to the iPhone and the iPad. In My Library, you can keep note

of your favorite workouts, create a workout routine, and save offline workouts.

Consider and initiate Meditations

1. Open the Fitness app on your iPhone, iPad, or Apple TV. Tap the Fitness+ icon if you are using an iPhone.
2. Select Meditation in the menu bar.
3. Choose among these:
- Select a Meditation session, then select Let's Begin to begin the session.
- Tap Filter, select a specific trainer, time, or topic, tap Done, tap a session, and then tap Let's Get Started.

Your Apple Watch displays the current time and heart rate during the Meditation. Swipe right to locate the icons to pause, restart, and terminate the Meditation. If you press the Workout button while Meditation is playing, you can begin a workout. Swipe to the left to access playback controls similar to those in the Music application.

If you pay for Apple Fitness+, you can use the Mindfulness app to listen to guided meditations on your Apple Watch.

Consider a workout program with multiple episodes.

1. Open the Fitness app on your iPhone, iPad, or Apple TV. Tap the Fitness+ icon if you are using an iPhone.
2. Select a program to view.

Each program tile displays the style of workout as well as the number of episodes in the program.

3. Choose among these:

- Get a preview peek: Click Watch the Film to watch a video describing the program's objectives and exercises.

- Tap the episode you wish to add to My Workouts, or tap  **+ ADD ALL** to add all episodes.

After selecting an episode from the selection, tap the button that initiates the workout.

- After you complete an episode, the next episode is automatically shown under Next Workout so you don't lose your place. Nevertheless, you are free to select any episode at any time.

Sort exercise routines

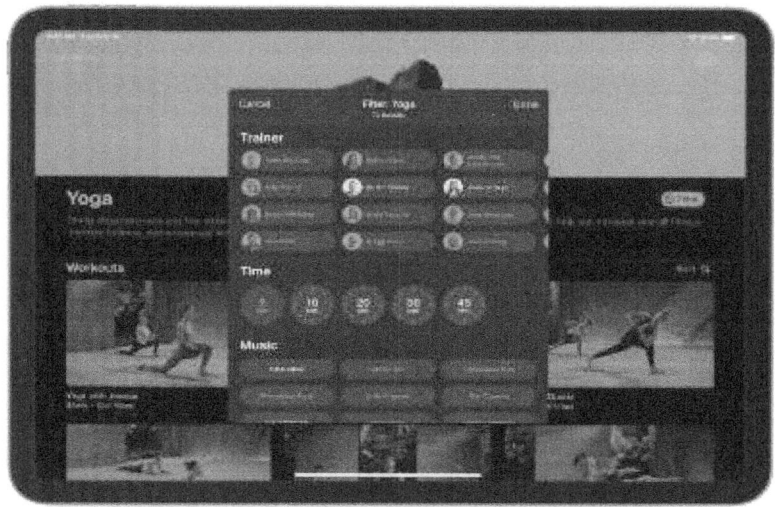

You can sort and filter specific workout types (such as Rowing and Dance) by trainer, workout duration, music genre, and more. This makes it easier to locate the desired exercise.

1. Open the Fitness app on your iPhone, iPad, or Apple TV. Tap the Fitness+ icon if you are using an iPhone.
2. Choose an exercise category, then perform one of the following:

- To sort workouts, tap Sort and then select an option such as Trainer or Time.
- Tap Filter, then select the desired filter(s).

If you are unable to choose a criterion, there are no workouts that match that filter.

Apple Fitness+ allows you to begin an exercise.

You can initiate an Apple Fitness+ workout from your iPhone, iPad, or Apple TV. Workouts on Apple Fitness+ are designed for individuals of all fitness levels, allowing you to challenge yourself whether you're just starting out or repeating the same routines. Every workout includes additional trainers who demonstrate how to modify the exercises to make the workout simpler or more difficult. Trainers may also instruct you on how to modify an exercise, such as substituting your body weight for dumbbells.

Users of the Apple iPhone or iPad can begin an exercise.

1. Start the fitness app. Tap the Fitness+ icon if you are using an iPhone.

If you do not already have it, you can obtain the Fitness app from the App Store.

2. Choose a workout type at the top of the screen, then choose a workout, or choose a workout from one of the categories (like Popular or Guest Trainer Series).

3. Choose among these:

- Add the workout to My Workouts by clicking **+ ADD** .

- Tap Preview to witness a workout preview.
  You can also view the playlist for the workout. If you have Apple Music, tapping Listen in Music will launch the playlist within Apple Music.

- Tap ▶ the start icon, then tap on your iPhone, iPad, or Apple Watch to initiate the exercise. When beginning a Treadmill workout, select Run or Walk for the most accurate data.

You can still begin a workout even if you're not wearing your Apple Watch, but your stats (such as calories expended) will not be recorded. To initiate the workout, select "Workout Without a Watch."

To stream your workout to a TV or HomePod that supports AirPlay 2.0, touch the display, tap again, and then select a destination.

Additionally, you can begin a workout on Apple TV.

Start a workout routine on Apple TV.

1. Launch the Fitness application, and then select who is working out.

2. Choose a type of exercise and then a specific exercise, or select an exercise from one of the categories.

3. Choose among these:

- To preview the workout, click Preview.

- Begin the exercise by clicking the "Free Trial" icon if you haven't already. If you have already signed up, select the "Start Workout" button.

- To obtain the most accurate stats, select Run or Walk when beginning a treadmill exercise.

- Select a song from the list of songs to launch the workout playlist in the Music app (Apple Music subscription required).

- View additional workouts: Scroll down until you see the Related Workouts row, then swipe left or right to view an additional workout.

Stop an exercise in Apple Fitness+ and restart it.

You can pause a workout on the device that is currently playing it or on your Apple Watch.

- On Apple Watch, perform any of the following:

- To end a workout, simultaneously press the side button and Digital Crown. Additionally, you can swipe left or right and then tap Pause side ⏸.

- To resume a workout, simultaneously press the side button and the Digital Crown, swipe right and tap Resume, or swipe left and tap the Play icon ▶ .

- Use your iPhone or iPad to perform any of the following:

- To pause a workout, tap the screen and then the Pause icon
  II.

- Tap the Play icon ▶ to continue a workout.

- On Apple TV, press the center of the clickpad (Siri Remote 2nd Gen) or the touch surface (Siri Remote 1st Gen) to halt or begin a workout. Tap the Siri Remote's ▶II Play/Pause icon.

Pause an Apple Fitness+ workout and review it.

You can pause a workout on the device where it's playing or on your Apple Watch.

Upon completion, you can share your exercise, cooldown, and other information.

- Swipe right and then select End on the Apple Watch.
  A summary of your practice is displayed. Tap "Done" to return to the Workout application.

- On your iPhone or iPad, touch ⊗ the End Workout button twice.

  A summary of your practice is displayed. Tap ➕ ADD to save the workout to My Workouts, tap to share it, tap Mindful Cooldown to select a cooldown workout, or tap Done to return to Apple Fitness+.

- On Apple TV, press the button using the Siri Remote or Apple TV Remote, followed by End Workout.

- A summary of your practice is displayed. Choose "Mindful Cooldown" to select a cool-down exercise, or "Done" to return to Apple Fitness+.

Chapter 9

Work out together using SharePlay

SharePlay powers Group Workouts, which let you work out with up to 32 of your best people. You can start a FaceTime call on your iPhone or iPad and then start a Group Workout using the Fitness app on your iPhone, iPad, or Apple TV.

Everyone on the call hears the workout at the same time, and each person can direct playback from their own device. This means that you and your friends can cheer each other on, see when someone closes an Activity ring, and get alerts when someone goes ahead of the pack on the Burn Bar during HIIT, Treadmill, Cycling, and Rowing workouts.

Group workouts with Apple Fitness+ require an iPhone, iPad, or iPod touch with iOS 15.1 or later and an Apple Watch Series 4 or later with watchOS 8.1 or later. To play video, Apple TV needs tvOS 15.1 or later. If you want to play on a Mac, you need macOS Monterey 12.1 or later. FaceTime, some FaceTime features, and other Apple services might not be available in all countries or regions, and the features might be different based on where you live.

Start a Group Workout with FaceTime on your iPhone or iPad.

1. FaceTime lets you call someone.

2. Open the Fitness app on your iPhone or iPad. Then, if you have an iPhone, tap the button for Fitness+.
   If you don't already have it, you can get the Fitness app from the App Store.

3. Choose a workout, start it, and then tap SharePlay to get everyone on the call to move. (Others on the call may need to tap Open when asked to use SharePlay in order to join the Group Workout.)

Everyone on the call who can hear it starts the workout at the same time. People who don't have access are asked to get it (through a subscription or, if offered, a free trial).

Using the playback settings on their own devices, like an Apple Watch, everyone can start or stop the workout.

Tap the X in the top left corner of the iPhone or iPad screen to stop a workout before it's done. Swipe the Apple Watch to the right, and then tap End.

Use the iPhone or iPad Fitness app to start a Group Workout.

1. Open the Fitness app on your iPhone or iPad. Then, if you have an iPhone, tap the button for Fitness+.
   If you don't already have it, you can get the Fitness app from the App Store.

2. Tap ●●● the button, choose a workout, and then tap SharePlay.

3. In the To field, type the names of the people you want to work out with. Then, tap FaceTime.

4. Tap Let's Begin when the FaceTime call comes in.

To join the workout, the recipient must tap the text of the workout at the top of the FaceTime controls and then tap Open. Everyone on the call who can hear it starts the workout at the same time. People who don't have access are asked to get it (through a subscription or, if offered, a free trial).

Using the playback settings on their own devices, like an Apple Watch, everyone can start or stop the workout.

Tap the X in the top left corner of the iPhone or iPad screen to stop a workout before it's done. Swipe the Apple Watch to the right, and then tap End.

You can join a group workout on Apple TV.

You can join a Group Workout on an Apple TV with SharePlay.

Note: SharePlay settings only appear when both Apple TV and FaceTime on an iPhone or iPad are signed in with the same Apple ID. Press and hold the TV button on the Siri Remote to switch users on Apple TV. This opens Control Center, where you can choose an existing user or add a new one.

1. Start a FaceTime call with an iPhone or iPad.
   Apple TV can tell when a FaceTime call is happening because a SharePlay icon appears in the upper-right area of the Home Screen.

2. Open the Fitness app on Apple TV and then do one of the following:

- Begin a workout, then when asked, choose SharePlay and confirm on your iPhone or iPad.

- To open Control Center, press and hold the TV button on the Siri Remote. Then, on your iPhone or iPad, tap the SharePlay button, choose Join, and confirm.

3. Go to Fitness, find a workout, and start it if you haven't already.

The workout is played at the same time on all the platforms on the FaceTime call, including Apple TV. Using the buttons on their own devices, everyone can play or pause the video in real time.

You can change what's on the screen during an Apple Fitness+ workout.

Change the numbers on screen

During your workout, you can look at your device to see how far you've gone on each of your rings, as well as your heart rate and how many calories you've burned.

Some workouts also show the Burn Bar, which shows how your metrics compare to those of other people who have done the same practice. The more calories you've burned, the further up the Burn Bar you are. In your workout summary, your position on the Burn Bar is saved along with your other exercise stats.

You can change the numbers that Apple Watch shows on the screen while you work out. The options for the Fitness app's metrics are the same on all of your devices where you've signed in with your Apple ID.

Note: Fitness+ subscribers who use AirPlay to watch their workouts can now see personal metrics from their Apple Watch on compatible screens in real time.

1. Tap when you work out.

When working out with Apple TV, move your hands in these ways:

- On the second-generation Siri Remote, press down on the clickpad ring or swipe down on the clickpad to see the Info bar. Then, click on the Metrics tab.
- Siri Remote (1st generation): Swipe down on the touch surface to open the Info pane, then move to the Metrics pane.

2. Choose one of the following:

- Turn off Show measures to stop all measures.
- Your data are still being tracked, but you can't see them.
- Change how time is shown by selecting "Off," "Show Time Elapsed," or "Show Time Left."
  Even if you turn off Time, the workout session timer will still be there.
- Stop the Burn Bar: Stop using the Burn Bar.

If you turn off the Burn Bar, your workouts won't count towards the group Burn Bar, and you won't be able to see where you stand when you're done.

Put on the closed captions and subtitles.

All Fitness+ workouts (SDH) have descriptions and subtitles for people who are deaf or hard of hearing. After you choose a workout, you can look below the time, type of music, and date it was added to see if it has closed captions and SDH.

- During a workout, on an iPhone or iPad, tap ⋯, then tap Subtitles, and then pick a language.

- During a workout, you can do one of the following with Apple TV, based on what kind of remote you have:
- Siri Remote (2nd generation): To open the Info pane, press down on the clickpad ring or swipe down on the clickpad. Then choose a language in the Subtitles pane.
- Siri Remote (1st generation): Swipe down on the touch surface to see the Info pane, then move to the Subtitles pane and choose a language.

iPhone or iPad users can download an Apple Fitness+ workout.

You can download workouts to your iPhone or iPad so you can work out even when you aren't online.

1. Open the app to get fit. Then, if you're using an iPhone, tap the Fitness+ button.
2. Choose one of these:

- Choose a workout, tap **+ ADD** to add it to My Workouts, and then tap   to save it on your computer.
- To see all of the workouts you've downloaded, go to the end of the Fitness+ tab and tap Downloaded.
  To start a downloaded workout, tap the one you want and then tap the button.
- To get rid of a downloaded workout, tap the downloaded workout, click   , and then tap Remove Download.

Note: You can't use the Burn Bar during recorded workouts.

With Apple Watch, you can keep track of what you do every day.

The Activity app ⊚ on your Apple Watch keeps track of how much you move during the day and pushes you to meet your fitness goals. The app keeps track of how long you work out, how often you stand, and how much you move around. Three different colored rings show how far you've come. By going through each ring every day, the goal is to move around more and sit less.

The Fitness app on your iPhone tracks how much you move around. If you've been tracking your movement for at least six months, it will show you daily trend data for active calories, exercise minutes, stand hours, stand minutes, walk distance, cardio fitness, walking pace, and more. Tap Summary in the Fitness app on your iPhone, and then scroll down to Trends to see how you're doing compared to how much you usually do.

Don't forget that your Apple Watch is not a medical tool.

Start off.

When you set up your Apple Watch, you are asked if you want to set up the Activity app. You can do it the first time you open the Activity app if you don't want to.

1. Open the Activity app ⊚ on your Apple Watch.
2. Swipe left to read about Move, Exercise, and Stand, and then tap Get Started.

138

3. The Digital Crown lets you set your gender, age, height, weight, and whether or not you use a wheelchair.

4. Choose an exercise level and get moving.

Check on your progress.

Open the Activity app on your Apple Watch to find out how you're doing at any time. On the Activity app, there are three rings.

- The red Move ring shows you how many calories you've burned by moving around.

- The green Exercise ring lets you know how many minutes you've spent moving quickly.

- The blue "Stand" ring tells you how many times you've stood up and moved for at least one minute per hour during the day.

If you use a wheelchair, the blue "Stand" ring turns to "Roll" and shows how many times you've rolled for at least one minute per hour during the day.

Turn the Digital Crown to see how much money you have right now. Keep scrolling to see a graph of your progress, as well as the number of steps, miles, workouts, and flights you've taken.

If the rings touch, you've reached your goal. Turn the Digital Crown and tap Weekly Summary to see how you're doing for the week.

Check out the report for the week.

1. Open the Activity app on your Apple Watch.
2. Move to the bottom of the screen with the Digital Crown, and then tap Weekly Summary.

In the summary, the total number of calories, the average number of calories, steps, distance, flights climbed, and active time for a week are given.

What you want to change.

If you think your exercise goals are too hard or not hard enough, you can change them.

1. Open the Activity app on your Apple Watch.
2. Move to the bottom of the screen with the Digital Crown, and then tap Change Goals.
3. To change a goal, touch or and then touch Next.

Every Monday, you find out what you got done the week before and can change your goals for the week ahead. Based on how well you've done in the past, your Apple Watch suggests new goals.

Think about what you've done so far.

1. Open the Fitness app on your iPhone, then tap Summary.

2. Tap the Activity area, then tap   the button, and then tap a date.

Check out what's happening.

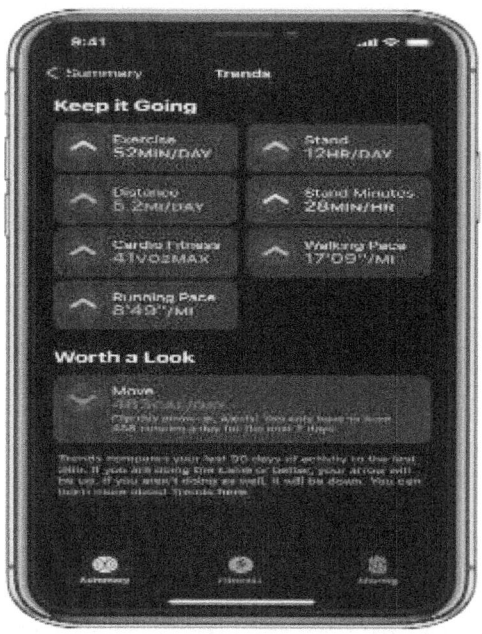

In the Trends area of the Fitness app on your iPhone, you can see how your active calories, exercise minutes, stand hours, walking distance, stand minutes, cardio fitness, walking pace, and running pace change every day. Trends looks at what you've done in the last 90 days and compares it to what you've done in the last 365.

Follow these steps to see how far you've come:

1. Open the Fitness app on your iPhone, then tap Summary.
2. Swipe up to find out what people like.
3. Tap Show More to learn how to stop a trend from happening.
4. When you tap a trend, you can see how it's changed over time.

If the Trend arrow for a certain metric goes up, it means that your fitness level is staying the same or getting better. If an arrow points down, it means that your 90-day average for that measure has started to go down. You will get advice like "Walk an extra quarter of a mile every day" to help you get inspired to change the trend.

Check out your awards.

You can get awards for personal goals, streaks, and big steps with your Apple Watch. Follow these steps to see all of your awards, including Activity Competition awards and awards you're working towards:

1. Open the Activity app on your Apple Watch.
2. The Awards screen is reached by making two swipes to the left.
3. Scroll down to find out what you won. Click on a gift to learn more about it.

You can also open the Fitness app on your iPhone, tap the Summary tab, and then swipe up to see the Awards at the bottom of the screen.

Take charge of reminders to do things

You can meet your goals with the help of reminders. Your Apple Watch tells you if you are meeting your exercise goals or falling behind. Follow these steps to decide what alerts and notes you want to see:

1. Open the Setting app on your Apple Watch.
2. Tap Activity, then set up the notifications.

Your iPhone can also be used. Open the Apple Watch app, tap "My Watch," then tap "Activity."

Stop giving lessons every day

To turn off activity reminders, do the following:

1. Open the Setting app on your Apple Watch.
2. Tap "Activity," then "Daily Coaching," and turn it off.

You can also open the Apple Watch app on your iPhone, tap My Watch, tap Activity, and then turn Daily Coaching off.

Share what you've done with your Apple Watch.

Telling your family and friends about your exercise plan can help you stick to it. You could also tell a teacher or trainer. You can find out when your friends reach their goals, finish their workouts, or win achievements.

You can add a friend or remove one.

If you've never shared your exercise before, open the Fitness app on your iPhone and tap Sharing. Tap Get Started, then do the following:

1. Open the Activity app on your Apple Watch.
2. Move to the bottom of the screen by swiping left and then turning the Digital Crown.
3. Tap "Invite a Friend" and then "Add a Friend."

To get rid of a friend, tap the friend you're sharing with and then tap Remove Friend.

Once a friend accepts your invitation, you can both see what they are doing and what they are doing to you. If a friend hasn't accepted an invitation, tap their name in the Invited area of the Sharing screen and then tap Invite Again.

To add a friend, you can also open the Fitness app on your iPhone, tap Sharing, tap , and then tap to send an email invitation or tap to send an invitation through Messages.

Note: If Apple manages your Apple Watch, open the Activity app, swipe left, tap Add Friends, and then tap the name of a friend.

See how your friends are doing.

1. Open the Activity app on your Apple Watch.
2. To move through your list of friends, swipe to the left and turn the Digital Crown.
3. Tap a friend to see what they did that day.

Try to do better than them.

A little good competition can keep you going. You can invite a friend to a competition in which you get more points the more Activity Rings you close. Every day that you add 1% to your rings, you get one point. The game lasts for 7 days, and you can get up to 600 points per day, for a total of 4,200 points for the week. The guy with the most points at the end of the race wins. During a battle, alerts tell you if you are ahead of or falling behind your competitor, as well as your score.

1. Open the Activity app on your Apple Watch.
2. Swipe to the left, tap a friend, and then tap Compete.
3. Tap Invite [your friend's name], and then wait for your friend to say yes.

Or, you can scroll down and tap Compete when you get an Activity sharing notice, such as when a friend just closed their rings or doubled their step goal.

You can also open the Fitness app on your iPhone, tap Sharing, tap a friend, and then tap Compete with [friend's name].

Change how your friends are set up.

You can easily change how friends use the app. Open the Activity app on your Apple Watch, swipe left, tap a friend, scroll down, and then do any of the following:

- Tap "Mute Notifications" to turn off alerts for the friend.
- To hide what you're doing from a friend, tap "Hide my Activity."
- Touch "Remove Friend" to get rid of the friend.

Apple Watch should have an alarm.

You can set your Apple Watch to make a sound or vibration at a certain time by using the Alarms app .

Say something like, "Set an alarm to go off every day at 6 a.m." to Siri.

You can set an alarm on Apple Watch.

1. Open the Alarms app on your Apple Watch.
2. Select Add Alarm.

   Tap AM or PM, then tap the hours or minutes.
3. You don't need to do this if you use 24-hour time.

4. Turn the Digital Crown to make changes, then tap .

5. Tap the switch to turn on or off the alarm. Or, you can tap the alarm time to get choices like repeat, label, and snooze.

Tip: Set an alarm that taps your wrist but doesn't make a sound by turning on quiet mode.

Don't allow yourself to sleep.

You can stop a clock for a few minutes by tapping "Snooze" when it goes off. If you don't want to let sleep, do these things:

1. Open the Alarms app  on your Apple Watch.
2. Tap the alarm in the list of alarms, and then turn Snooze off.

Delete an alarm

1. Open the Alarms app  on your Apple Watch.
2. Choose one from the list.

Scroll to the bottom, then tap the Delete button.

Skip an alarm clock

If you usually wake up at a certain time, you can skip your alarm for just that night.

1. Open the Alarms app ⏰ on your Apple Watch.

2. Tap the clock that appears under Sleep | Wake Up, and then tap Skip for Tonight.

See the same alarms on both your iPhone and Apple Watch

1. Set an alarm on your iPhone.

2. Open the Apple Watch app on your iPhone.

3. Tap "My Watch" and then "Clock." Turn on Push Alerts on your iPhone.

Your Apple Watch tells you when an alarm goes off so you can snooze it or turn it off. (Your iPhone won't tell you when your Apple Watch's alarms go off.)

Set up Apple Watch as an alarm clock by your bed.

1. Open the Setting app ⚙ on your Apple Watch.

2. Go to "General" and then "Nightstand Mode." Then turn "Nightstand Mode" on.

When nightstand mode is on and your Apple Watch is plugged into its charger, it shows the charging state, the current time and date, and the time of any alarms you've set. Tap the screen or gently nudge your Apple Watch to see the time. Even if you nudge or tap the table, it might work.

If you use the Alarms app to set an alarm, your Apple Watch will gently wake you up with its own alarm sound while it is in bedside mode.

When the alarm goes off, you can turn it off by hitting the side button or press the Digital Crown to put it to sleep for 9 minutes.

Press to snooze.

Press to turn off alarm.

Books on tape could be added to the Apple Watch.

Apple Watch can be synced with ebooks from Apple Books.

Note: Audiobooks from other sources can't be synced with Apple Watch.

1. Open the Apple Watch app on your iPhone.
2. Click My Watch, then click Audiobooks.

Tap "Add Audiobook," and then pick the audiobooks you want to add to your Apple Watch.

If there's enough space, your Apple Watch instantly syncs the entire contents of the audiobook you're listening to and the one listed under "Want to Read." If there's room, your Apple Watch also downloads five hours of each audiobook you add. Audiobooks sync to the Apple Watch when it is charged.

Audiobooks can be played on an Apple Watch.

Using the ebooks app on your Apple Watch, you can play ebooks from Apple Books.

On Apple Watch, you can listen to podcasts.

1. Connect your Apple Watch to headphones or speakers that use Bluetooth.
2. Open the Audiobooks app on your Apple Watch.
3. To move through the art, turn the Digital Crown.
4. Touch a book to make it talk.

You can listen to books on tape from the library.

You can stream audiobooks from your audiobooks library to your Apple Watch if it is near your iPhone or linked to a Wi-Fi network (or a cellular network, if you have an Apple Watch with cellular).

1. Open the Audiobooks app  on your Apple Watch.
2. Tap Library, then tap the book you want to listen to.

You can also play audiobooks that were bought from Apple Books by other people in your Family Sharing group. On the Audiobooks screen, tap My Family, and then tap a book.

Siri can play audiobooks.

You can use Siri to play a podcast from your library.

"Play "In the Time of the Butterflies" on an audiobook."

Change the music.

Turn the Digital Crown to change the sound. These tools can be used to play audiobooks:

Play the audiobook.

Pause playback.

Skip ahead 15 seconds.

Skip back 15 seconds.

Playback speed. Options include 1x, 1 1/4x, 1 1/2x, 1 3/4x, 2x, and 3/4x.

Choose a track or chapter.

Chapter 10

Measure blood oxygen levels on Apple Watch

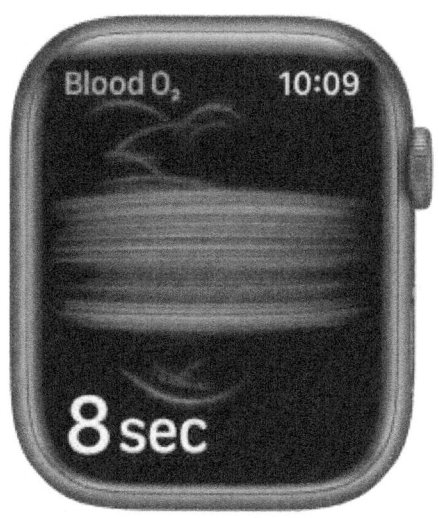

Using the Blood Oxygen app ⟳ on an Apple Watch Series 6 or later, you can determine how much oxygen your red blood cells transport from your lungs to the rest of your body. Knowing how well your blood is oxygenated can help you determine your overall health and wellness.

Note that the Blood Oxygen app is not available everywhere. The Blood Oxygen app's measurements are not intended for use in medicine.

Establish Blood Oxygen

1. On your Apple Watch, launch the Settings application ⚙.

2. Select Blood Oxygen, then activate Blood Oxygen Measurements.

When Sleep Focus or theater mode is enabled, background measurements are disabled.

For blood oxygen measurement, a bright red light glows against the wrist. This might be simpler to see at night. You can switch off the measurement lights if they are bothersome.

1. On your Apple Watch, launch the Settings application .
2. deactivate In Sleep Focus and In Theater Mode.

Determine the amount of oxygen in your circulation.

If background measurements are enabled, the Blood Oxygen app performs multiple daily blood oxygen level tests. Additionally, you may obtain measurements whenever you desire.

1. On your Apple Watch, launch the Blood Oxygen application.
2. Place your arm on a table or in your lap and ensure that your forearm is flat, with the Apple Watch's display facing up.
3. Press Start and hold your arm still for 15 seconds as the timer counts down.
4. When the measurement is complete, the results are obtained. Tap Finish.

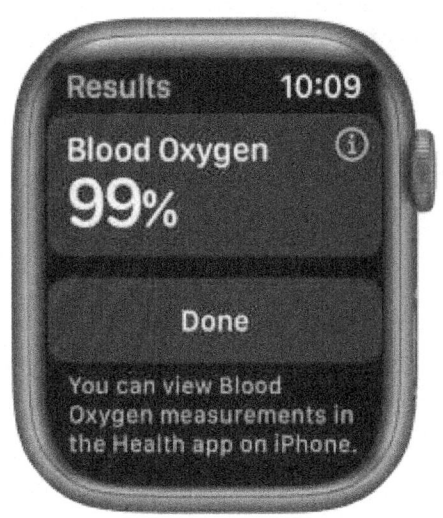

Note: You must contact the back of your Apple Watch with your skin. Blood Oxygen readings will be more accurate if your Apple Watch is neither too tight nor too loose and allows your epidermis to breathe.

Examine your Blood Oxygen measurement history.

1. On your iPhone, launch the Health application.
2. Select Browse followed by Respiratory and Blood Oxygen.

Use the Apple Watch calculator

With the Calculator app , you can perform basic mathematical operations. Additionally, you can rapidly determine how much to tip and how to split the bill.

Siri: Say, "How much is 18 percent of 225?" or "What is 73 times 9?"

Perform a fast calculation.

1. On your Apple Watch, launch the Calculator application .
2. Tap the numbers and operators to obtain the answer.

Divide the bill and determine how much to tip

1. On your Apple Watch, launch the Calculator application .
2. Enter the total quantity of the bill, then tap Tip.
3. 3.Turn the Digital Crown to select the tip amount.
4. Select People, then rotate the Digital Crown to input the number of individuals who will be splitting the bill.

You can see the amount of the tip, the total bill, and how much each individual owes if the bill is divided evenly.

Please note that the Tip function is not always accessible.

If you uninstall the Calculator app from your iPhone, it will be removed from your Apple Watch as well.

The Apple Watch allows users to view and modify their calendar.

The Calendar app  on your Apple Watch displays planned and invited engagements for the next six weeks and two years (in List and Day views). The Apple Watch can display events from any or all of your iPhone's calendars.

Say something to Siri such as "What's my next event?"

Apple Watch allows users to view their calendar.

1. Launch the Calendar app on your Apple Watch or touch the date or a calendar event on the watch face.
2. Turn the Digital Crown to view an upcoming schedule.

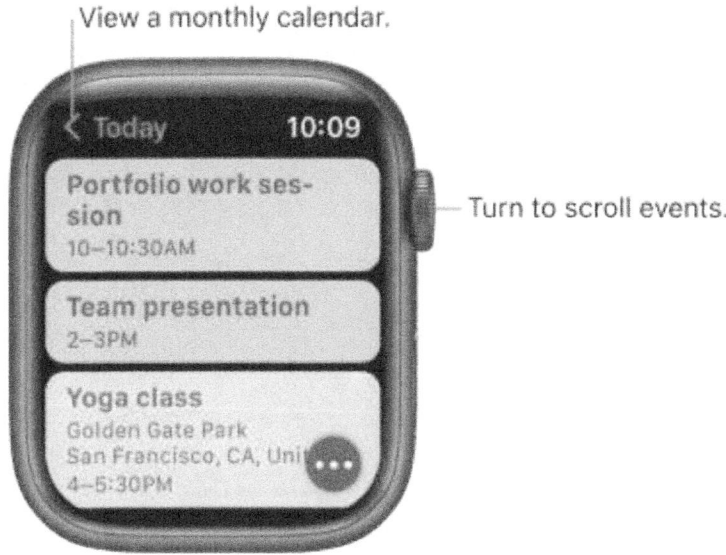

View a monthly calendar.

Turn to scroll events.

3. Tap on an event to see more information about it, such as the time, location, status of invitees, and notes.

Tap the in the upper left corner to advance to the next event.

You can also view this week's and this month's events.

Change your perspective on things.

Launch the Calendar application on your Apple Watch, tap, and then touch a new view.

- Up Next: Displays upcoming events for the next week.
- Day: Only displays events occurring on this day.
- List: Displays all of your events from the previous two weeks to the following two years.

If you are in Day view, swipe left or right, and if you are in List view or Up Next view, turn the Digital Crown.

To return to the current day and time, tap the time in the upper-right quadrant of the display.

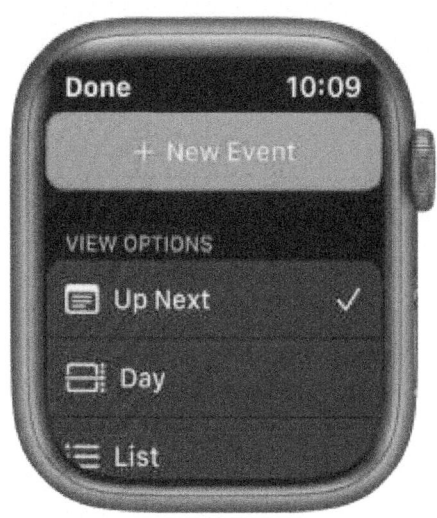

View months and periods

While viewing events in Day or List view, you can toggle between week and month perspectives. After launching the Calendar app on your Apple Watch, you can perform the following:

- Display the week number: Tap the button in the upper-left quadrant of the screen.
- Select a different week: Swipe left or right.
- Display what is occurring during a specific week: Tap a date on the week's calendar.
- Show the current month: While the current week is displayed, tap the upper left corner of the screen.
- Select a different month: Move the Digital Crown with your mouse.
- Choose a week from the month's calendar: Consider the week.

Add an occasion

By default, your Apple Watch will communicate with the calendar events you create on your iPhone. Additionally, you can schedule events on your watch.

- Apply Siri: Say something like, "Add a FaceTime with Mom event to your calendar for May 20 at 4 p.m."
- Using the Apple Watch Calendar app, tap and then press New Event when viewing events in Up Next, Day, or List view. Include the event's title, description, date, and time, as well as a list of those who are invited. Select the calendar to which you wish to add the event, then select Add.

Remove or modify an event

- To cancel an engagement you created: Tap an event, then tap the Delete button twice.
  If this is a recurring event, you can eliminate this specific occurrence or all future occurrences.
- Use the Calendar app on your iPhone to modify an event.

Respond to an invitation in Calendar

You can respond to event invitations on your Apple Watch immediately or later.

- Scroll to the bottom of the notification and tap Accept, Decline, or Maybe if you receive an invitation.
- If you discover the notification later, select it in your list of notifications, scroll, and then respond.
- If you are already in the Calendar app, you can respond by tapping the event.

To contact an event organizer, tap the organizer's name in the event's information, then press the phone, message, or Walkie-Talkie button.

Find out how to get to an event

If an event has a location, your Apple Watch can direct you there.

1. On your Apple Watch, launch the Calendar application.
2. Click on an event, followed by the address.

Modify "leave now" messages

If an event contains a location, your Apple Watch sends you a "leave now" notification based on how long it will take you to get there and how congested the roadways are. To select a specific time frame, such as two hours prior to the event, perform the steps below:

1. Launch the iPhone's Calendar application.
2. Select the event.

3. Touch the Alert icon, then choose a different time.

Change the calendar's parameters

Change the type of calendar notifications you receive and select which calendars to display on Apple Watch by following these steps:

1. On your iPhone, launch the Apple Watch application.
2. Select My Watch followed by Calendar.
3. Tap Custom under Notifications or Calendars.

Apple Watch can be used as a camera remote and a timer.

If you want to position your iPhone for a photo from a distance and then take the photo, you can use your Apple Watch to see what the iPhone camera sees and then take the photo. Additionally, you can set a shutter timer on your Apple Watch. This allows you to remove your hand from the camera and gaze up during the shot.

Your Apple Watch must be within normal Bluetooth range of your iPhone (approximately 33 feet or 10 meters) for it to function as a camera remote.

Siri: "Take a picture," or similar command.

Take a picture

1. On your Apple Watch, launch the Camera Remote application.

2. Use your Apple Watch as a viewfinder to compose your iPhone photograph.

3. Turn the Digital Crown to zoom in or out.

4. To adjust the exposure, touch the subject of the image on the Apple Watch's preview display.

5. Tap the Shutter icon to capture a photo.

The image is saved to the Photos app on your iPhone, but you can view it on your Apple Watch.

Review your photos

Follow these instructions to view photos on your Apple Watch.

- To view an image, tap the thumbnail in the bottom-left corner.
- Examine other images: Swipe left or right.
  Zoom by turning the Digital Crown.
- Pan: Move a zoomed-in image horizontally.
- To fill the display, tap the image twice.
- Hide or display the Close button and shot count: Tap the screen.

When finished, press the Close button.

Choose a different camera and adjust its settings.

1. On your Apple Watch, launch the Camera Remote application .

2. Tap, then select one of the options:

- Timer (on or off for a 3-second timer);

- Camera (forward or aft)
- Flash (auto, enabled, or disabled)
- A live image (auto, enabled, or disabled)
- HDR (enabled or disabled)

Chapter 11

Use the Compass app on Apple Watch

The Compass application ⊕ displays your location, altitude, and the direction your Apple Watch SE or Apple Watch Series 5 or later is facing. On the Apple Watch SE and Apple Watch Series and later, you can set Compass Waypoints, discover the distance and direction between them, and use Backtrack to trace your steps.

If you uninstall the Compass application from your iPhone, it will also be removed from your Apple Watch.

Determine your bearing, height, slope, and coordinates.

The center of the face of the timepiece indicates your direction. By rotating the Digital Crown, you can view your incline, elevation, and coordinates in the interior ring of the compass. Continue scrolling to see where your waypoints are located.

Tap ☰ the upper left corner of any compass view to view details as a list.

1. On the Apple Watch, launch the Compass application ⊕ .

2. To add a bearing, tap ☰ , scroll down, tap Bearing, and then tap Done.

To change the bearing, tap ▤, scroll down, touch Bearing, and then turn the Digital Crown to the new bearing.

3. To clear the bearing, tap ▤, scroll down, and then select Clear Bearing.

Note that coordinates may not be accessible in all areas.

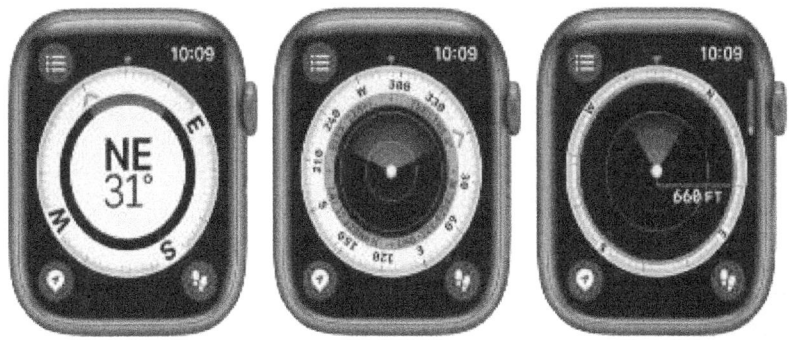

Create waypoints and display them.

Using the Compass app on an Apple Watch SE, Series 6, or later with watchOS 9, you can designate your current location as a waypoint. Then, you can determine the distance and direction between each Compass Waypoint.

1. On the Apple Watch, launch the Compass application ⚲ .

2. To add a waypoint, tap ◈ it.

3. Enter the waypoint's name, color, or symbol (such as "car" or "home"), and then select "Done."

4. To view a Compass Waypoint, touch a waypoint on any of the three Compass displays, rotate the Digital Crown to select a waypoint, and then press the Select button.
   On the screen, the distance and direction to the destination are displayed, such as "3.7 miles to your left."
5. Tap the screen's bottom to view the waypoint's coordinates on a map.

Tap  the waypoint interface to modify the information for a specific waypoint.

Add the Compass Waypoint feature to the watch face (only available for Apple Watch SE and Apple Watch Series 8).

Using a Compass Waypoint complication, you can easily reach waypoints you've created, the most recently viewed waypoint in the Compass app, or your parked car.

1. Touch and hold the display while the watch face is active, and then select Edit.
2. Swipe left until the end is reached.
6. If a visage has issues, they will be displayed on the final screen.
3. Tap a complication to select it, then turn the Digital Crown to Compass Waypoints and take one of the subsequent actions.
- To add a complication, tap one of the first three waypoints.
- Tap "More," then tap a waypoint, the "Last Viewed" waypoint, or the "Parked Car" waypoint.
4. Tap the face to switch to it, then press the Digital Crown to save your modifications.
5. Tap the complication to display the waypoint in the Compass app.

Review your previous actions.

The Compass app on an Apple Watch SE, Series 6, or later with watchOS 9 can monitor your route and assist you in retracing your steps if you become disoriented.

Backtrack is intended for use away from familiar locations, such as your home or office, and in crowded areas without Wi-Fi.

1. On the Apple Watch, launch the Compass application  .

2. Touch  and then touch Start to initiate route recording.

3. Select  and then select Retrace Steps to return to your previous location.

   On the compass, the initial press  location is displayed.

4. Return along the path to the point where you first activated Backtrack.

5. Once complete, tap  and then select Delete Steps.

Add elevation functionality to the watch face (Apple Watch SE and Apple Watch Series 8).

On the Apple Watch Series 6 and later, the altimeter is always on, allowing you to monitor your elevation in public in real time. Add the elevation feature to the watch face so that you can quickly determine your altitude.

1. Touch and hold the display while the watch face is active, and then select Edit.

2. Swipe left until the end is reached.

   If a visage has issues, they will be displayed on the final screen.

3. Tap a complication to select it, then tap Elevation after turning the Digital Crown to Compass mode.

4. Tap the face to switch to it, then press the Digital Crown to save your modifications.

If Location Services is disabled, Compass will not display height or coordinates. Open the Settings app on your Apple Watch, tap Privacy, and then select Location Services to turn Location Services on or off.

To use true north instead of magnetic north, open the Settings app on your Apple Watch, select Compass, and then toggle the Use True North switch. On the settings tab for Compass, you can also select a grid system. You have the option of selecting DMS, decimal degrees, MGRS/USNG, or UTM.

Note: Some watch straps are composed of magnetic materials that can interfere with the compass.

Contacts

In the Contacts app, you can view, amend, and share contacts from other devices with the same Apple ID. You can also contribute your own information to a contact card and create contacts.

Examine your contacts on the Apple Watch.

1. On the Apple Watch, launch the Contacts application .

2. Move through your contacts by rotating the Digital Crown.

3. Touch a contact to view their information and notes.

If the contact has an image, you can touch it to make it larger.

Talk to your contacts.

You can call, text, email, or initiate a Walkie-Talkie conversation from the Contacts app.

1. On the Apple Watch, launch the Contacts application .
2. Move through your contacts by rotating the Digital Crown.
3. Tap a contact, then perform any of the following actions:

*   Tap the contact's name to view their phone number. Tap a number to contact it.

*   Tap to access an existing message thread or to create a new one.

*   Tap to begin composing an email.

*   Tap the person's name to invite them to Walkie-Talkie or, if they've accepted and have Walkie-Talkie turned on, to initiate a Walkie-Talkie conversation.

Establish a contact

1. On the Apple Watch, launch the Contacts application.
2. Tap New Contact after performing a downward swipe.
3. Enter the individual's name and, if desired, their company.
4. Tap Done after entering a phone number, email address, and address.

You can share, edit, and delete a contact.

1. On the Apple Watch, launch the Contacts application .
2. Move through your contacts by rotating the Digital Crown.

3. Tap a contact, then navigate down and select Share Contact, Edit Contact, or Delete Contact.

Utilize the Apple Watch's Cycle Tracking function

Using the Cycle Tracking app, you can keep track of your menstrual cycle. You can record information about your flow and symptoms such as migraines and cramps. The Cycle Tracking app can tell you when it believes your next period or fertile window is about to start based on the information you've entered. Cycle Tracking can make more accurate predictions by combining your heart rate data with the information you've already inputted. If you wear your Apple Watch Series 8 to bed every night, the app can use your wrist temperature to determine when you ovulated in the past and when your period will begin.

Note: The Health app is designed to protect your information and allow you to choose what to share.

Implement cycle tracking.

1. On your iOS device, launch the Health app.
2. To access the Health Categories interface, tap Browse in the bottom-right corner.
3. Tap Cycle Tracks.
4. Follow the on-screen instructions to configure notifications and other options after tapping Get Started.

To add or remove options for Cycle Log, open the Health app on your iPhone, tap Browse, tap Cycle Tracking, and then tap Options next to Cycle Log.

The Apple Watch can record your cycle.

1. On your iOS device, launch the Cycle Tracking app.
2. Tap the buttons and select the options that best describe your period, such as the quantity of blood and symptoms.

Your observations will appear in the iPhone's Cycle log. If you have enabled Period Notifications and Fertility Notifications in the Health app on your iPhone, you will receive notifications about imminent periods, fertile window predictions, and, on the Apple Watch Series 8, estimates of when you ovulated in the past.

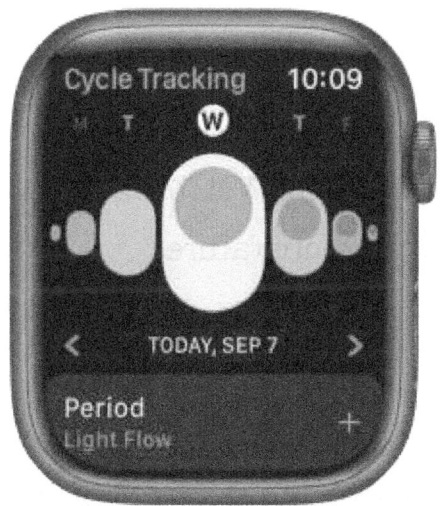

On an iPhone, you can also use the Health app to monitor cycle-altering factors such as pregnancy, breastfeeding, and birth control. Depending on your settings, your iPhone and Apple Watch may cease predicting your period, fertile window, and ovulation from the past (on Apple Watch Series 8).

The Cycle Tracking application should not be used to prevent pregnancy. You should not use data from the Cycle Tracking app to diagnose your health issues.

The Apple Watch Series 8 allows you to monitor temperature fluctuations.

Changes in body temperature may indicate that a woman has ovulated. When worn while sleeping, the Apple Watch Series 8 can monitor temperature fluctuations and use this data to improve period prediction and estimate ovulation after the fact.

Important: The temperature sensor is not a medical device and should not be used for medical diagnosis, treatment, or any other purpose.

Monitor your wrist's temperature.

1. Configure Sleep and Cycle Monitoring.
2. Enable Sleep Focus and wear your Apple Watch while you sleep in order to obtain a baseline temperature.
   After approximately five nights, wrist temperature data will be available.
3. To view wrist temperature data, launch the Health app on your iPhone, tap Browse, tap Body Measurements, and then press Wrist Temperature.

You should be able to estimate when you ovulated after two cycles.

Your body temperature naturally fluctuates, and it can vary from night to night contingent on a variety of factors. The temperature of your wrist can also be affected by factors such as your sleeping environment.

Stop measuring the temperature of your wrist

1. Open the Health app on your iPhone, hit Browse, and then tap Cycle Tracking.
2. Tap Options, followed by Disable Wrist Temperature.

If you disable wrist temperature monitoring, you will no longer receive estimates of when you ovulated in the past, nor will your wrist temperature be used to determine when your period will begin.

Apple Watch's ECG app is used to record an electrocardiogram.

You can generate an electrocardiogram (ECG) using the ECG app
and an Apple Watch Series 4 or later with an electrical heart rate sensor. To use the ECG app, you must update your iPhone 8 or later to the most recent version of iOS and your Apple Watch to the most recent version of watchOS. The ECG app is not available on the Apple Watch SE, and it is not universally accessible.

1. Launch the Health application on your iPhone, and then follow the on-screen prompts to configure ECG.
   If you do not see a setup prompt, tap Browse in the lower right corner, select Heart, and then select Electrocardiogram (ECG).
2. Use your Apple Watch to launch the ECG application.

3. Arm yourself with a table or your chest.

4. Use the hand that is not holding the watch to press the Digital Crown. Then, Apple Watch will record the ECG.

During the session, the Digital Crown is not required to be pressed.

At the conclusion of the recording, you will be graded. After that, you can select your symptoms by tapping Add Symptoms. Tap Save to record your symptoms, and then tap Done. To view your results (ECG), open the Health app on your iPhone, tap Browse in the bottom-right corner, then tap Heart > Electrocardiograms.

Important: Clean and dry your Apple Watch after swimming, taking a shower, perspiring heavily, or washing your hands for the finest reading. Your Apple Watch may require at least one hour to fully dry. ECGs are designed to function between 0° C and 35° C (32° F to 95° F).

Apple Watch can help you navigate or contact a friend.

Use Find People to rapidly determine how to reach a friend's residence.

Inform an acquaintance how to reach a destination.

1. On your Apple Watch, launch the Find People application.

2. To open the Maps app , tap your friend, scroll down, and hit Directions.

3. Tap the route to receive turn-by-turn directions from your current location to your friend's location.

Discuss with a companion.

1. On your Apple Watch, launch the Find People application.

2. To call, email, or text a friend, select the contact, scroll down, and then tap Contact.

Apple Watch can locate misplaced devices.

Using the Find Devices app on Apple Watch, you can locate Apple devices that you have misplaced or left behind. To locate your Apple devices, you must link them to your Apple ID.

Determine where something is.

If your device is online, the Find Devices application can pinpoint its location. Find Devices is able to locate supported devices even if they are off, in Low Power Mode, or in airplane mode.

Launch the Find Devices app  on your Apple Watch, then select the target device.

- If it is possible to locate the device, its location is visible on the map. Above the map, you can view the device's distance, its last Wi-Fi or cellular connection, and its remaining battery life. Below the map is an approximate location.
- If the device cannot be located, "No location" will appear next to the device's name. Turn on Notify When Found in the Notifications section. When it is located, you will be notified.

You can broadcast a sound using your iPhone, iPad, iPod touch, Mac, or Apple Watch.

1. Launch the Find Devices app on your Apple Watch, then tap a device.

2. Select the Play sound button.

- If the machine is online, a sound begins after a brief delay and progressively becomes louder for approximately two minutes. The machine (if applicable) vibrates. The screen of the device displays a "Find My [device]" message.

- Your Apple ID email address will also receive an email of confirmation.

- If the device is not connected to the internet, you will see "Sound Pending." The sound will play once the device reconnects to a Wi-Fi or cellular network.

Use your AirPods or Beats headphones, play a song.

If your AirPods or Beats headphones are connected to your Apple Watch, you can play a sound on them using Find Devices.

On supported AirPods models, you can even play a ringtone while they are in their case.

1. Launch the Find Devices app on your Apple Watch, then tap a device.

2. Select the Play sound button. If you lose your AirPods or AirPods Pro, you can disable one by swiping to the left or right.

- If the device is connected to the internet, it immediately emits a two-minute sound.

In addition, your Apple ID email address will receive a confirmation email.

- If the device is not connected to the internet, you will receive a notification the next time it is in range of your Apple Watch.

Determine how to reach a device.

Using the Maps app on your Apple Watch, you can obtain directions to the current location of a device.

1. Launch the Find Devices app on your Apple Watch, then select the device for which you desire directions.
2. To bring up Maps, tap Directions.
3. Touch the route to receive directions from your current location to the device's location.

Receive a warning when you forget a device.

When you leave your device behind, you can receive a reminder so you don't lose it. You can also set Trusted Locations, which are places where you can leave your device without receiving a warning.

1. Launch the Find Devices app on your Apple Watch.
2. Tap the device you wish to set up a notification for.
3. Under Notifications, tap Notify When Left Behind, and then enable Notify When Left Behind.

Additionally, you can open the Find My app on your iPhone, tap Devices, touch the device for which you wish to configure a notification, and then tap Notify When Left Behind. Enable "Notify When Left Behind" and then follow the on-screen instructions.

To add a Trusted Location, select one of the suggested locations or tap New Location, select a location on the map, and then tap Done.

Mark an item as missing

If your iPhone, iPad, iPod touch, Apple Watch, or Apple TV gets lost or stolen, you can switch on Lost Mode or lock your Mac.

1. Launch the Find Devices app on your Apple Watch, then tap a device.
2. Tap Lost Mode, then toggle Lost Mode on.

When a missing device is reported, the following occurs:

- An email confirmation is sent to your Apple ID email address.
- A message indicating that the device has been lost and how to contact you appears on the Lock Screen of the device.
- Your device does not display alerts or make sounds when you receive messages, notifications, or an alarm. You can still receive FaceTime and phone communications on your device.
- Your device does not support Apple Pay. Your device deletes any Apple Pay credit or debit cards, student ID cards, or Express Transit cards. Your credit, debit, and student ID cards are removed even if your device is inactive. When your

device reconnects to the Internet, Express Transit cards are removed.

- On a map, you can view the current location of your iPhone, iPad, iPod touch, or Apple Watch as well as its location history.

Find Items allows you to locate an AirTag or other item.

You can use the Find Items application on your Apple Watch to locate a misplaced AirTag or third-party item associated with your Apple ID.

See where something is located.

Launch the Find Items application on your Apple Watch, and then select the item you wish to locate.

- If the item can be located, it will appear on the map so that it can be located. Above the map, you can view the device's distance, its last Wi-Fi or cellular connection, and its remaining battery life. Below the map is an approximate location.

- If you cannot locate an item, you can view its last known location and time. Under Notifications, tap Notify When Found, and then enable Notify When Found. You will be notified when it is located again.

To produce a sound or a noise.

If the object is nearby, you can play a sound to assist you locate it.

Note: If an item cannot play a sound, the Play Sound option will be absent.

1. Launch the Find Items app on your Apple Watch, then select the object for which you wish to play a sound.
2. Select the Play sound button.

To halt a sound from playing, tap halt Sound before it automatically stops.

Find out where something is

You can obtain directions to the current or last known location of an item using the Maps app on your Apple Watch.

1. Launch the Find Items app on your Apple Watch, then select the item for which you desire directions.
2. To bring up Maps, tap Directions.

3. Click the route to obtain directions from your current location to the item's location.

Receive a notification when you leave something behind.

When you leave an item behind, you can receive a notification so you don't misplace it. You can also configure "Trusted Locations," which are locations where you can leave your item without receiving a notification.

1. On your Apple Watch, launch the Find Items application .

2. Touch the item for which you wish to set up an alert.

3. To activate Notify When Left Behind, tap Notify When Left Behind.

Additionally, you can open the Find My app on your iPhone, tap Items, touch the item for which you wish to set up an alert, and then tap Notify When Left Behind. Enable "Notify When Left Behind" and then follow the on-screen instructions.

To add a Trusted Location, select one of the suggested locations or tap New Location, select a location on the map, and then tap Done.

Find Items on Apple Watch enables users to report a misplaced AirTag or other item.

Mark an item as lacking

You can designate a lost AirTag or other third-party item associated with your Apple ID with the Find Items app.

1. Tap on an item after launching the Find Items app on your Apple Watch.

2. Tap Lost Mode, then toggle Lost Mode on.

If someone discovers your item and connects to it, they can obtain additional information.

Take an artifact out of Lost Mode

When you have located what you were searching for, disable Lost Mode.

1. Launch the Find Items application on your Apple Watch, and then select the item.

2. Touch Lost Mode, then disable Lost Mode.

Apple Watch displays your heart rate

Keeping an eye on your heart rate is a good method to monitor the health of your body. You can view your resting, walking, exercise, and post-workout heart rates, as well as your heart rate during a Breathe session, and you can take a new reading at any time.

Note: Both your wrist and Apple Watch should be free of dirt and moisture. Water and perspiration can degrade the sound quality of an audio recording.

Check your pulse rate

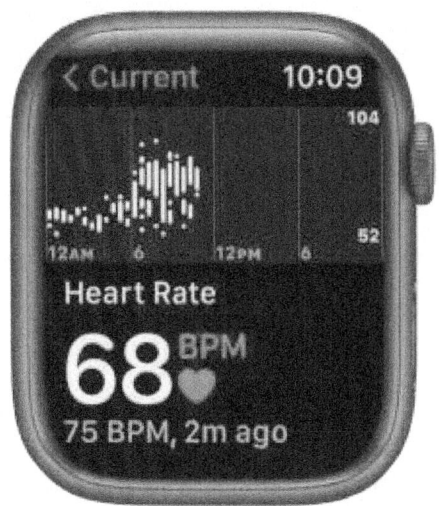

Open the Heart Rate application on your Apple Watch to view your current heart rate, resting heart rate, and walking heart rate average.

As long as the Apple Watch is worn, it will monitor your heart rate.

Examine a graph depicting your heart rate.

1. On your Apple Watch, launch the Heart Rate app.
2. Touch Current, Resting Heart Rate, or Walking Average to view your average heart rate throughout the day.

To view your heart rate data over an extended period, launch the Health app on your iPhone, tap Browse, tap Heart, and then tap an entry. You are able to view heart data from the previous hour, day, week, month, or year.

Heart rate data must be enabled.

Apple Watch's Heart Rate app, workouts, and Breathe and Reflect sessions monitor your heart rate by default. If you have disabled heart rate data, you can enable it again.

1. On your Apple Watch, launch the "Settings" app .

2. Go to Health under Privacy and Security.

3. Tap Heart Rate then toggle Heart Rate on.

Heart Rate can also be enabled by opening the Apple Watch app on your iPhone, tapping My Watch, Privacy, and then Heart Rate.

Note: For features such as wrist detection, haptic notifications, blood oxygen level measurements (on Apple Watch Series 6, Apple Watch Series 7, and Apple Watch Series 8) and the heart rate sensor, the back of your Apple Watch must contact your skin. Fitting your Apple Watch correctly—not too snug, not too loose, and with space for your skin to breathe—keeps you comfortable and allows the sensors to function properly.

Heart Health

The Apple Watch can monitor your heartbeat and alert you if something is wrong. For instance, your Apple Watch can notify you if your resting pulse rate remains above or below a certain threshold for at least 10 minutes.

You can enable heart rate notifications the first time you launch the Heart Rate app, or at any time thereafter.

You can also receive a notification if your Apple Watch detects atrial fibrillation (AFib). If you are already aware that you have AFib, your Apple Watch can help you determine how often this irregular cardiac rhythm occurs. You can also monitor events that may have an impact on your health.

Receive alerts if your heart rate is too high or too low.

1. Open the Settings app on your Apple Watch and then tap Heart.

2. Tap High Heart Rate Notifications or Low Heart Rate Notifications, and then designate a heart rate threshold.

Open the Apple Watch app on your iPhone, tap "My Watch," then touch "Heart." Touch High Heart Rate or Low Heart Rate and then set a threshold.

Receive notifications regarding an irregular heartbeat (not available in all regions).

If Apple Watch detects an irregular pulse that appears to be atrial fibrillation (AFib), it can send you a notification.

1. On your Apple Watch, launch "Settings."

2. Tap Heart, then toggle Irregular Rhythm Notifications on.

Additionally, you can launch the Apple Watch application on your iPhone, tap My Watch, tap Heart, and then touch Irregular Rhythm.

AFib history (not available in all regions).

1. Open the Health app on your iPhone and then tap Browse if you have been diagnosed with AFib.

2. Follow the on-screen instructions after tapping Heart, scrolling down to Get More Out of Your Health, tapping Set Up under AFib History, and then tapping Heart again.

3. To view your AFib history, launch the Health app, tap Browse, tap Heart, and then press AFib History.

If you have worn your watch for at least 5 out of 7 days (12 hours a day), you may get a message on Monday with an estimate of how much time you spent in AFib the week before.

Receive alerts when your cardio fitness is insufficient.

Apple Watch can estimate your cardio fitness by measuring how hard your pulse is working when you walk, run, or hike outside and alerting you when it falls below a certain threshold. Depending on your age and gender, your cardio fitness will fall into one of four categories: Low, Below Average, Above Average, or High. If your cardio fitness level falls below the "Low" threshold, your

Apple Watch will notify you. If it remains low for four consecutive months, you'll receive an alert.

1. On your Apple Watch, launch "Settings."
2. To enable Cardio Fitness Notifications, navigate to Heart and touch Cardio Fitness Notifications.

You can also open the Apple Watch app on your iPhone, select My Watch, tap Heart, and then enable Cardio Fitness Notifications.

The "Cardio Fitness" section of the Health app displays your cardio fitness measurements and the range in which they occur.

Apple Watch allows for household control.

The Home app provides a secure method of controlling HomeKit-enabled devices such as lighting, locks, smart TVs, thermostats, window shades, and smart plugs. On supported devices, you can also send and receive Intercom messages and view the video feeds of HomeKit Secure Video cameras. All Apple Watch controls are located on the forearm.

When you first launch the home app 🏠 on your iPhone, the setup assistant will assist you in creating a residence. Then, you can configure scenes, designate rooms, and add HomeKit-enabled devices. On your Apple Watch, you can utilize the same accessories, scenes, and chambers that you add to your iPhone.

You might say to Siri, "Turn off the lights in the office," or "Turn off the lights in the office."

Examine your home's condition.

The Home app 🏠 displays the status of the presently active devices. For instance, it may indicate that the thermostat is set to a particular temperature or that the front door is accessible. Simply touch a button to learn more about the accessory or to control it.

1. Utilize your Apple Watch to launch the Home application 🏠 .

2. Tap any of the circular icons directly beneath your home's name.

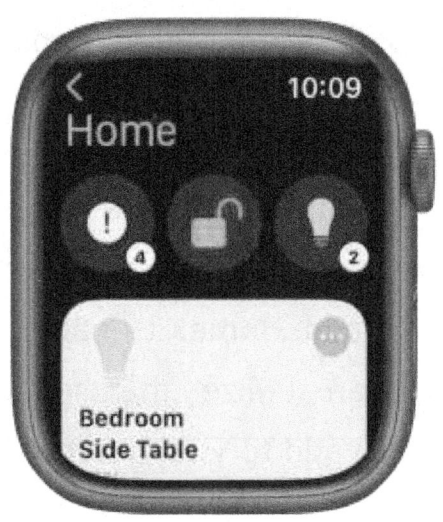

When multiple accessories are displayed in a status, you can control each accessory or group of accessories by touching the status. For example, if all the lights are on in the living room and bedroom, you can select the status and then turn off only the lights in the living room.

Manage the smart home's gadgets and scenes

When you activate the Home app on your Apple Watch, the appropriate scenes and accessories are displayed near the top of the screen. For instance, a coffee maker may be present in the morning and a bedside lamp in the evening.

Scroll up and then tap Cameras, Favorites, or a room to see the remainder of your accessories.

Choose one of the options below to operate an accessory:

- Activate or deactivate an accessory: Tap the accessory, such as a light or home key, to unlock a lock that is compatible with it.

- Modify the settings of an accessory: Tap  for additional options. Tap "Done" to return to the list of accoutrements. The available controls depend on the type of accessory. Some light bulbs, for instance, have controls for adjusting both luminance and color. Slide left to view additional controls.

- Take command of your favorite room accessories: touch Favorites or a room, then touch an accessory or tap to modify its settings.

- To view a camera's live video feed, select Cameras and then a camera.

Launch the scene by launching the Home app 🏠 on your Apple Watch and tapping the scene.

Examine a distinct house.

If you have multiple homes configured, your Apple Watch allows you to choose which one to view.

Launch the Home application 🏠 on your Apple Watch, and then:

- Tap the home icon if the Home Screen is visible.
- If a particular home is displaying, tap and then touch another home.

Apple Watch permits the sending and receiving of Intercom messages.

Using the household app 🏠 on Apple Watch, you can send Intercom messages to everyone in your household. You can also send communications to specific rooms or areas via the intercom.

1. Utilize your Apple Watch to launch the Home application 🏠
   .
2. Slide downward and then press the Intercom button.
3. Inquire, "Who ate the last piece of pizza?"
4. Tap Finish.

A recording of your voice is sent to all the HomePod speakers in your home and to the iOS, iPadOS, and watchOS devices of everyone who can send and receive Intercom messages in your home.

Raise your Apple Watch and say something like, "Hey Siri, tell the office, "The movie is starting," or "Hey Siri, tell the upstairs, "I'm going to the store."

Control your connected home devices with your Apple Watch.

If you have an Apple TV (3rd generation or later) or HomePod in your household, you can use your iPhone and a paired Apple Watch to control HomeKit-enabled accessories. The Apple TV or HomePod functions as a hub for your home and allows you to communicate with your devices remotely.

Permit access from a distance.

On your iPhone, navigate to Settings > [your name] > iCloud, then activate Home. Ensure that the identical Apple ID is used on each device.

If both your iPhone and Apple TV are signed in with the same Apple ID, they will be seamlessly paired.

Read mail on Apple Watch

You can read email on your Apple Watch and reply using the QWERTY and QuickPath keyboard (not available in all languages, only on Apple Watch Series 7 and Apple Watch Series 8), dictation, Scribble, emoji, or a prepared response. Alternatively, you can switch to your iPhone to compose a response.

A message alert that notifies you of incoming correspondence.

1. When you receive a new communication, you simply need to raise your wrist.

2. Swipe down from the top or touch "Dismiss" at the bottom of the alert to dismiss it.

Swipe down on the watch face to see the list of unread alerts and touch it there if you miss the notification.

To change the manner in which your Apple Watch displays email notifications, launch the Apple Watch app on your iPhone, select My Watch, and then navigate to Mail > Custom.

Use Mail to access your email.

1. Launch the Mail application on the Apple Watch.
2. Turn the Digital Crown to navigate the message list.
3. Tap a message to view it.
4. To move to the beginning of a lengthy message, rotate the Digital Crown or touch the screen's top.

The way messages are set up makes them simple to read on your Apple Watch. The majority of text styles are preserved, and you can tap website URLs in Mail to view content optimized for the Apple Watch and the web. Double-tap the screen to magnify its contents.

Links to websites may not be accessible everywhere.

Tip: If you select a phone number, address, or link in an email, you can dial the number, view a map, or view web-formatted content.

Use an iPhone.

Follow these steps to view an incoming message on your iPhone:

1. Start your iPhone up.
2. On an iPhone with Face ID, swipe up from the bottom edge and pause to access the App Switcher. The App Switcher can be accessed by double-clicking the Home button on an iPhone.

3. Tap the icon at the bottom of the screen to launch Mail.

Apple Watch can send and receive email

Publish an announcement

1. Launch the Mail application 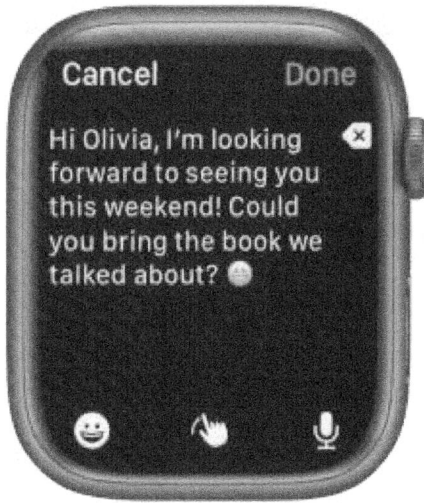 on the Apple Watch.
2. Utilize the Digital Crown to navigate to the top of the display, and then select "New Message."
3. Tap Add Contact to add a recipient, tap From to select an account to send from, tap Add Subject to create a subject line, and then tap Create Message to send the email.

If your Apple Watch is configured to use multiple languages, touch Language, select a language, and then tap the Create Message field.

Create a message.

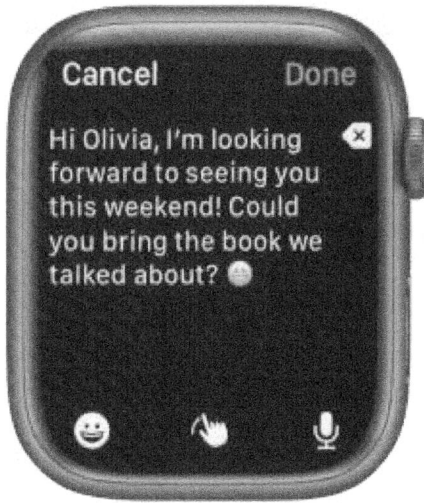

There are numerous methods to compose a message, the majority of which require only one screen. Tap the "Create Message" field and then perform one or more of the following:

- Utilize the QWERTY keyboard and QuickPath: (Not available in all languages; exclusive to Apple Watch Series 7 and Series 8). Use the QuickPath keyboard to navigate from one letter to the next without lifting your finger. Raise your index finger to conclude a word.

  A list of plausible words appears as you type. Additionally, you can select a completed or incomplete word to highlight it, then rotate the Digital Crown to see suggestions. Stop rotating the Digital Crown to access the highlighted suggestion.

  Swipe up from the bottom and touch the Keyboard button if the keyboard is not displayed.

- Utilize Scribble. Use your finger to write your message. To modify your message, use the Digital Crown to transfer the cursor to the desired location, and then make the desired modifications.

  Tap a completed word to highlight it, then turn the Crown to view suggested words. Stop rotating the Digital Crown to access the highlighted suggestion.

  Tip: If your Apple Watch is configured to use multiple languages, you can alternate between them when using Scribble. You can choose a language by scrolling up from the bottom of the screen.

Not all languages are supported by Scribble.

- To dictate text, tap 🎤 , state what you want to say, and then tap Done. You can also pronounce punctuation marks aloud, such as "did it arrive?"

  To reactivate Scribble, rotate the Digital Crown or touch 👆 the screen.

- Include emoji: Tap 😊 and then select a frequently used emoji or a category at the bottom of the screen. Scroll through the images to view them. When you locate the symbol you wish to include in your message, tap it.

- Type text with your iPhone: When you begin composing a message and your paired iPhone is nearby, a notification appears on the iPhone offering to allow you to type text using the iOS keyboard. Tap the notification, then compose the message on the iPhone.

Apple Watch allows you to reply to a message

Scroll to the bottom of a received message in the Mail app ✉, then select Reply. Tap Reply All if multiple recipients are receiving the message. Tap Add Message, then select one of the options below:

- Open the Apple Watch application on your iPhone, touch My Watch, navigate to Mail > Default Replies, and then tap Add reply. To modify the default responses, tap ⊖ Edit, drag to reorder them, or tap to remove one.

Scroll down, tap Languages, and then touch a language if none of the intelligent responses are in the desired language. The iPhone's Settings > General > Keyboard > Keyboards menu allows you to select the language you wish to use.

- enter a response: Tap the field labeled "Add Message," and then enter a response.

Open the email on the iPhone.

1. If you prefer to use your iPhone to respond, bring it up and then launch the App Switcher. (On an iPhone with Face ID, swipe up and halt from the bottom edge; on an iPhone with a Home button, double-click the Home button.)

2. Tap the button at the bottom of the screen to access the email in Mail.

Use Apple Watch to check your email

Choose which mailboxes to display on your Apple Watch.

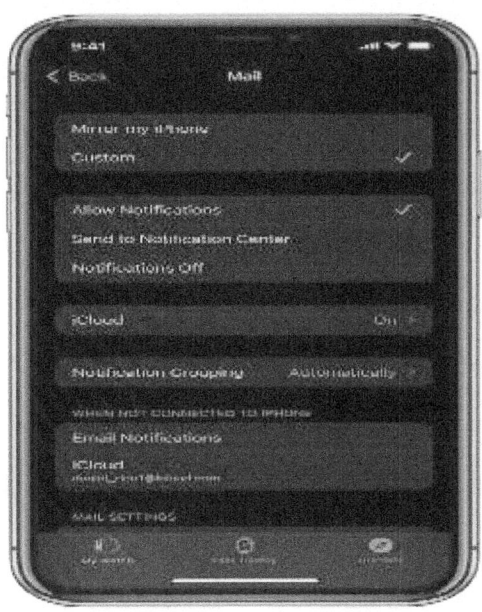

1. On your iPhone, launch the Apple Watch application.

2. Tap "My Watch," followed by "Mail," and then "Include Mail."

3. Tap the accounts you want to see on your Apple Watch under Accounts. You can select multiple accounts, such as iCloud and your work account.

4. You can select an account and then individual mailboxes to view their contents on your Apple Watch, if desired.

By default, messages from all inboxes are displayed. You can also select to view messages from VIPs, messages that have been marked, unread messages, and more.

You can also select which accounts and mailboxes to view on Apple Watch. Open the Mail application , navigate down and select Edit, then select an account or mailbox.

Apple Watch permits access to specific accounts

1. Launch the Mail application 📧 on the Apple Watch.
2. To view a list of accounts and special mailboxes, such as Flagged and Unread, tap the upper-left corner.
3. Tap a mailbox or account to view the contents.

Tap All Inboxes to view all of your email messages simultaneously.

Delete, mark as read or unread, or flag a message.

Open the Mail app 📧 on your Apple Watch, select a message, and navigate to:

- To mark a message as read ✉️ or unread ✉️, select "Mark as Not Read" or "Mark as Read."
  Swipe right on the message you wish to peruse, then tap the peruse or Unread button.
- To delete a message, tap Delete Message.
- If you are looking at the list of messages, swipe left on the message you want to read and then tap 🗑️ .
- To mark a message as important, tap Flag. (You can also remove an already set indicator from a message.)

If you are looking at the list of messages, swipe left on the message you want to read and then tap 🏳️ .

When you swipe a message thread, the action you select (Trash, Flag, Read, or Unread) applies to the entire thread.

Customize notifications

1. On your iPhone, launch the Apple Watch application.

2. Tap My Watch, navigate to Mail > Custom, tap an account, and then toggle Show Alerts from [name of account] to the on position.

3. Turn sound and touch on or off.

When an essential message arrives, you can also receive a notification on your Apple Watch, even when you're not near your iPhone. Launch the Apple Watch app on your iPhone, then select My Watch and Mail. Activate Email Notifications under When Not Connected to iPhone.

Reduce your message list

Reduce the number of preview text lines displayed for each email in your mailing list to make each message more condensed.

1. On your iPhone, launch the Apple Watch application. Tap "My Watch," followed by "Mail," then "Message Preview."

2. Choose to display either one, two, or no lines.

Download images remotely

Some communications may contain links to Internet-based images. If you allow images from external websites to display, those images will appear in the email. Follow the steps below to permit these images:

1. On your iPhone, launch the Apple Watch application.

2. To load remote images, select "My Watch," "Mail," "Custom," and "Load Remote Images."

Note: If you load images from a distance, it may take longer for your Apple Watch to download emails.

Sort items by threads.

Follow these steps to view all of an email's replies in a single thread:

1. On your iPhone, launch the Apple Watch application.

2. Choose "My Watch," "Mail," "Custom," and "Organize by Thread."

Apple Watch can help you locate and visit locations.

The Maps application on your Apple Watch allows you to view your surroundings and obtain directions.

Say something similar to:

- "Where exactly am I?"
- Find a coffee shop near me."

Examine the map.

1. On your Apple Watch, launch the Maps app .

2. Tap Search, and then tap to write or speak . The Apple Watch Series 7 and Apple Watch Series 8 also support the QWERTY and QuickPath keyboards (not available in all languages).

Note: Scribble is not supported in all languages.

Find nearby services.

1. On your Apple Watch, launch the Maps app 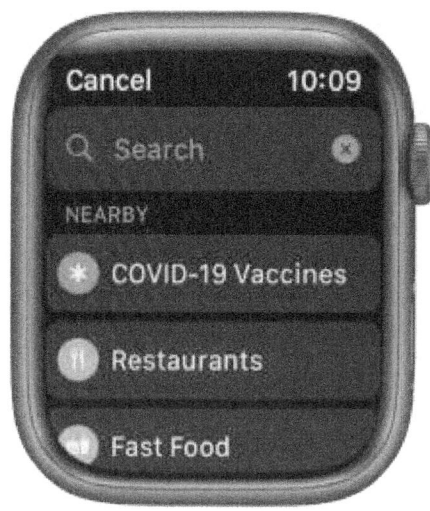 .
2. Tap, followed by tapping a category such as Restaurants or Parking.
3. Tap a result, then rotate the Digital Crown to navigate the information.
4. Tap the upper left corner to return to the results list.

Not everywhere has recommendations for nearby activities.

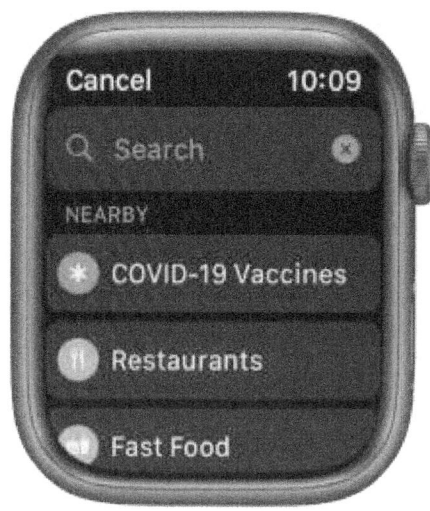

Consult a guide

1. Launch the Maps application on your iPhone, tap the search field, and swipe upwards.
- Select a cover that appears under City Guides or Guides We Adore.
- Touch Explore Guides, then touch a cover after perusing the guides.

- Select an entry under Browse by Publisher, and then select a cover.

2. Swipe up and tap ┼ next to the name of a location, such as a restaurant or park.

3. Select the guide to which you wish to add the location, or select "New Guide."

4. Launch the Maps app ⓐ on your Apple Watch, scroll down, and tap the guide to which you added the location.

Not all regions have guidebooks available.

Determine where you are and investigate the surrounding area.

1. On your Apple Watch, launch the Maps app ⓐ .
2. Select Location.
3. Tap and then tap Search Here to search for things near your current location.

Tap Transit Map to view nearby public transportation.

Note that Transit Map is not accessible in all areas.

On Series 5 and later Apple Watches, a cyan cone on the map indicates the direction your watch is facing.

Scroll and magnify

- To navigate the map, drag with one finger.
- Move the Digital Crown to zoom in and out on the map.
- You can double-tap a location on the map to magnify it.
- To return to your current location, tap the bottom right corner.

Find out about a landmark or place with a sign.

1. Tap the marker on the map to indicate your current location.
2. Turn the Digital Crown to navigate the available information.
3. Tap the upper left corner to return to the map.

Tip: To call a place, tap the phone number in the information about that place. Open the App Switcher to switch to your iPhone. (On an iPhone with Face ID, swipe up from the bottom edge and stop;

on an iPhone with a Home button, double-click the Home button.)
To open Phone, tap the button at the bottom of the screen.

Place, move, and take away map pegs

- To drop a pin, touch and hold the map where you want the
  pin to go, wait for the pin to descend, and then let go.
  Tap the blue dot and then tap Mark My Location to place a
  pin where you are.

- To move a pin, tap and hold it, then drag it or place a new
  pin where you want it to go.

- To get rid of a pin, touch it to see the address, scroll with the
  Digital Crown, and then tap Remove Marker.

Tip: Drop a pin on a location on the map, then select the pin to
see address information.

Check out recent locations

1. On your Apple Watch, launch the Maps app .

2. Scroll down and tap a place below "Recents."

You can also place guides you just looked at on your iPhone in Recents.

Find your path with Apple Watch

Siri: Ask: "How do I get to the local gas station?" "How do I get home?" "How far is it to the airport?"

Get directions

1. On your Apple Watch, launch the Maps app .
2. Turn the Digital Crown to navigate to Favorites, Guides, and Recents.
3. Tap an entry to get directions by car, on foot, by bus, or by bike.
   Note that not all forms of transportation are available in every place.
4. touch a mode to see suggested routes, then touch a route to start your trip and see an overview of it, including turns, the distance between turns, and street names.

In the top-left corner, you can see when you're anticipated to arrive. When you tap the arrival time, you can see how long it will take to get to your destination.

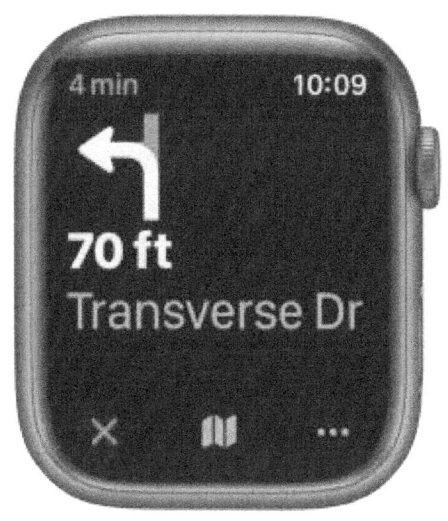

Tip: When you choose Cycling, you can see a summary of how the route's elevation changes. Tap to find out what kind of roads you'll be cycling on, such as whether they have bike lanes, are side roads or main roads, or require you to get off your bike and walk.

Check out how to get there.

With the Maps app, you can see suggested routes and choose between them before you start.

- Pick a different route: If more than one route shows up, tap one to follow it.
- Change to a route you can drive, walk, ride public transportation, or bike: Tap Walking, Driving, Public Transportation, or Biking.
- If you want to avoid tolls or highways, select > next to the address of your destination and then turn on an option.
- If you want to avoid hills or busy roads, select > next to the address of your destination and then turn on an option.

- Choose your preferred public transportation: When a transit route is shown, tap > and then choose the form of public transportation you want to use, such as a bus, subway and light rail, commuter rail, or ferry.

Determine how to reach a location or a map pin.

1. On your Apple Watch, launch the Maps app  .
2. Select Location, then select the desired location's landmark or map pin.
3. Scroll through the location details until you reach "Directions." Then, select whether you wish to walk, drive, utilize public transportation, or ride a bicycle.
4. When you're set to depart, tap a route and then follow the instructions.

Ask Siri a question such as, "How long will it take me to get home?""

Use maps for navigation.

Apple Watch can help you remain on track in a variety of ways, including the following:

- Turn the Digital Crown to view upcoming turns, and swipe the top of the screen to return to the previous one.

  Note: Location services must be enabled to use turn-by-turn directions. To enable or disable location services on Apple Watch, navigate to Settings ⚙️ > Privacy & Security > Location Services.

- Open a map: When looking at a list of turn-by-turn directions, tap to open a map that reveals where the turn is. You can zoom in and out of the map by turning the Digital Crown. Tap ▌▌▌ to go back to the list of turns.

- Listen for directions. Once you begin the first leg of your journey, your Apple Watch will tell you when to turn with sounds and taps. A low tone followed by a high tone (tock tick, tock tick) means to turn right at the next intersection; a high tone followed by a low tone (tick tock, tick tock) means to turn left.

  Open the Apple Watch app on your iPhone, tap My Watch, touch Maps, and then toggle the Driving, Driving with CarPlay, Walking, and Cycling alerts you would like to receive.

Tap ✕ the bottom-left corner of the display to cancel directions before you arrive, or tap ●●●, navigate down, and then tap End.

Apple Watch medication management

You can keep track of the drugs, vitamins, and supplements you take with the Health app on your iPhone. You can keep track of your medicines and get reminders on your Apple Watch by using the medicines app.

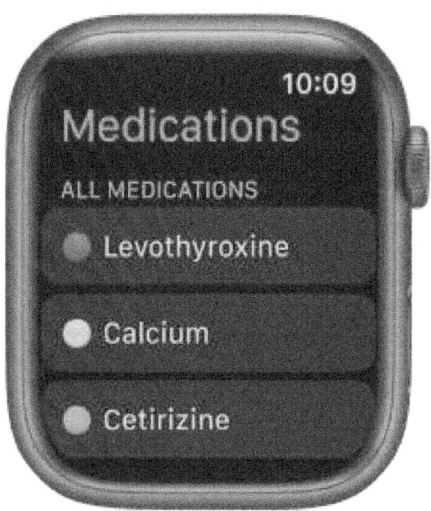

Note: The Medications feature should not be used instead of getting help from a doctor. More information is on the labels of your medicines, but you should talk to your doctor before making any choices about your health.

Create a medication schedule on your iPhone

1. Launch the Health application on your iPhone, tap Browse in the lower-right corner, and then touch Medications.
2. To add a medication to your list, click "Add Medication" or "Add a Medication."
3. To determine what substance it is, you can do one of the following:

- Tap the search field, type the name, and then tap the "Add" icon.
  Only in the United States do suggestions appear as you enter. You can select a suggestion or continue typing the name before tapping Add.
- Use the camera: (Only in the United States; on iPhone SE (2nd generation and later), iPhone XS, and iPhone XR) Tap next to the search field and then adhere to the on-screen instructions.

Tap Search by Name, then enter the name (as described above) if no match is found.

4. Follow the on-screen instructions to establish an identifier, set a schedule, and identify possible interactions.

List your medications

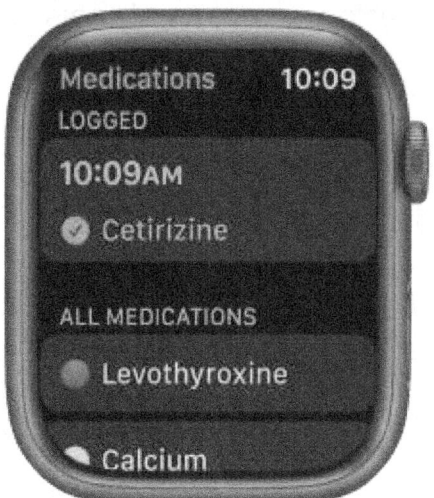

Follow these methods to manage your medications.

1. If you have been reminded to record your medications, tap the reminder; otherwise, launch the Medications app on your Apple Watch.

2. Examine your current medication schedule, such as the medications you take in the morning.

3. Tap Log All as Completed.
   Apple Watch keeps note of how much you took, how many units you took, and when you took the medicine.

4. Tap a medication under "Your Medications," then tap the "Log" icon.
   Under Logged, the medication's name and the time it was logged are displayed.

5. 5.To alter the status of a logged medication, tap it, then tap Taken or Skipped, followed by Done.

Open the Health app on your iPhone, press Browse, and then tap Medications to view your medication log and history.

Apple Watch allows you to check your messages.

You can read incoming text messages directly on your Apple Watch and respond using the QWERTY and QuickPath keyboard (not available in all languages and only on Apple Watch Series 7 and Apple Watch Series 8), dictation, Scribble, or a prepared response.

Apple Watch: View a text message

1. When your Apple Watch vibrates or makes a sound to alert you of a message, raise it to your face to read it.
2. Rotate the Digital Crown to access the final portion of the message.
3. To access the top of the message, tap the top of the screen.

If you select a link to a website within a message, you can view content that is formatted for the web and optimized for Apple Watch.

Touch and hold the top of the screen, swipe down to reveal the message notification, and then press it. Scroll down and tap Dismiss to mark the message as read. Press the Digital Crown to dismiss the notification without marking the message as read.

Verify when messages were sent

Tap a conversation in Messages ⭕ list of conversations, then swipe left on a message within that conversation.

Delete or mute a message.

- To mute a conversation, swipe left on the conversation in the list of conversations within Messages, then tap 🔕 .
- Swipe left on the conversation in the list of conversations in Messages, then tap 🗑 to delete it.

A message can contain images, music, audio, and video.

Messages can contain photos, videos, and audio files. To access them from your Apple Watch, follow these steps:

- Tap the photo to view it, double-tap it to fill the screen, and drag it to reposition it; then, tap the button in the upper left corner to return to the conversation.

  If you want to share the photo, tap it, then tap Messages or Mail. Scroll past the sharing options and tap Save Image to save the photo to the Photos app on your iPhone. Alternatively, tap Create Watch Face to add the photo to a Kaleidoscope or Photos watch face.

- Audio excerpt: Tap the clip to listen.

  The audio remains for 30 days, but you can set your iPhone to retain it for longer: Navigate to Settings, tap Messages, scroll to Audio Messages, tap Expire, and then tap Never.

- Music: If someone sends you Apple Music music through Messages, you can open and listen it in the Music app on Apple Watch by tapping the song, album, or playlist in the message.

- Tap on a video in a message to begin playing it in full screen mode. Tap once to display the playback controls. To zoom out, double-tap the display, and turn the Digital Crown to adjust the volume. To return to the conversation, swipe or tap the Back icon.

To save the video, view the message in the Messages application on your iPhone and save it there.

Choose how to obtain information.

1. On your iPhone, launch the Apple Watch app.
2. Click My Watch, followed by Messages.

3. Select "Custom" to configure how you wish to be notified when you receive a message.

If your Focus does not support Messages notifications, you will not receive a notification.

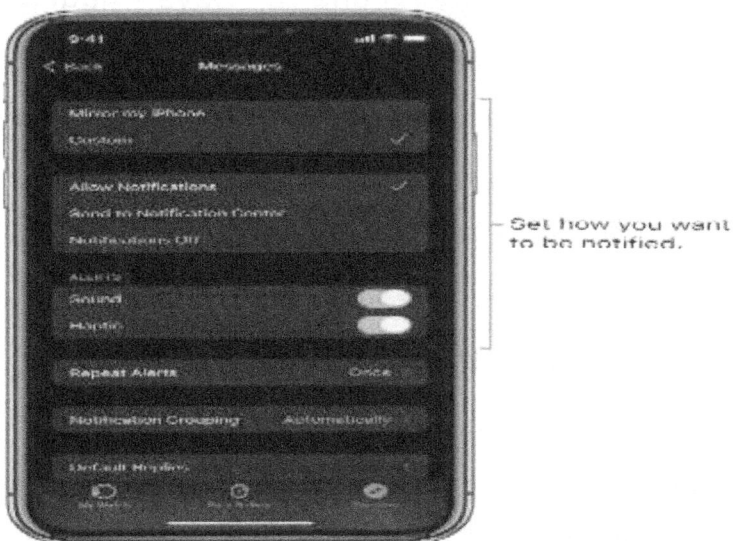

Apple Watch can send message

In the Messages app on your Apple Watch, you can compose and send messages containing text, images, emoji, Memoji stickers, and audio recordings.

Apple Watch allows users to transmit messages.

1. Use your Apple Watch to launch the Messages app .
2. Scroll to the screen's top and tap "New Message."
3. Tap "Add Contact," then tap a contact from the list of recent conversations, or select an option:

- Tap 🎤 to search for a contact or dictate a phone number.

- Tap 👤 to view a comprehensive list of your contacts.

- To add a phone number, tap ⊞ .

1. Tap the Create Message button.

2. If your Apple Watch is configured to use multiple languages, tap Language and then select a language.

Write a message via text

There are multiple methods to compose a message, but the majority of them can be accomplished on a single screen. After composing a message, tap the Create Message field and then do one or more of the following:

- Use the QuickPath keyboard to advance from one letter to the next without lifting your finger. Lift your finger to complete a word.

  As you type, word suggestions appear. You can also tap a completed or incomplete word to highlight it, then turn the Digital Crown to see suggestions. Stop rotating the Digital Crown to select the highlighted suggestion.

  If the keyboard is not visible, swipe up from the bottom and then touch the Keyboard button.

- Use Scribble: To edit your message, turn the Digital Crown to move the cursor to the desired location, and then make the desired modification.

To use predictive text, touch a completed or incomplete word to highlight it, then rotate the Digital Crown to see suggestions; stop rotating to select the highlighted suggestion.

Tip: If you have configured your Apple Watch to support multiple languages, you can switch languages when using Scribble by swiping up from the bottom of the screen and selecting the desired language.

Not every language supports Scribble.

- Tap 🎤 , utter your message, and then tap Done. You can also discuss punctuation. For instance, you could say, "Did it arrive, question mark?"

  Tap 👆 or rotate the Digital Crown to return to using Scribble.

- Add emoji to your message by tapping, tapping 😀 a frequently used emoji, or tapping a category, and then scrolling through the images until you locate the appropriate symbol.

- Enter text with your iPhone: When you begin composing a message and your paired iPhone is nearby, a notification appears on the iPhone offering to let you enter text using the iOS keyboard.

Send a clever response, a sticker, a Memoji sticker, a GIF, or an audio recording.

You can also compose messages without inputting any text. After sending a message, you can choose from the following options:

- Send an intelligent reply: Scroll down to see a list of useful phrases you can use, then select one, followed by Send.
  To add a custom response, open the Apple Watch app on your iPhone, tap My Watch, navigate to Messages, then Default Replies, and tap Add Reply. To modify the default responses, press Edit, then drag to reorder them or tap ⊖ to remove one.
  In Settings > General > Keyboard > Keyboards, you can select which languages your iPhone can use.

- Tap ⚓, tap 👤, tap an image from the collection of Memoji Stickers, tap a variant, and then press Send to send a Memoji sticker.

To transmit a sticker, tap ⚓, tap 👤, scroll to the bottom, and then tap "More Stickers." Tap a sticker, then tap transmit.

To send a GIF, tap ⚓, tap 🔍, and then tap Send. To locate a GIF, tap the Search field, type a search term, tap a GIF that appears, and then tap Send.

Tap ⚓, tap 𝄃𝄃𝄃, record what you want to say, tap Done, then press Send to send an audio clip.

Apple Cash allows you to send and receive funds.

1. During a conversation, tap ⚡ beside the iMessage field.

2. Tap 🅐Cash .

3. Select the quantity you wish to send using the Digital Crown, then tap Send.

4. To submit, double-click the side button.

Apple Cash is not available in all locations.

Send a sketch of an Apple Watch

You can use Digital Touch to send sketches to contacts who have an Apple Watch or an iPhone with iOS 10 or later.

If a sketch is sent to you, you can select the notification to view it.

1. compose a message, followed by tapping ⚡.

2. To access the drawing canvas, tap ♡ it.

3. Draw on the display with your finger.

4. Select a different color by tapping the dot in the upper-right quadrant.

5. When you are finished sketching, touch "Done" followed alien "Send."

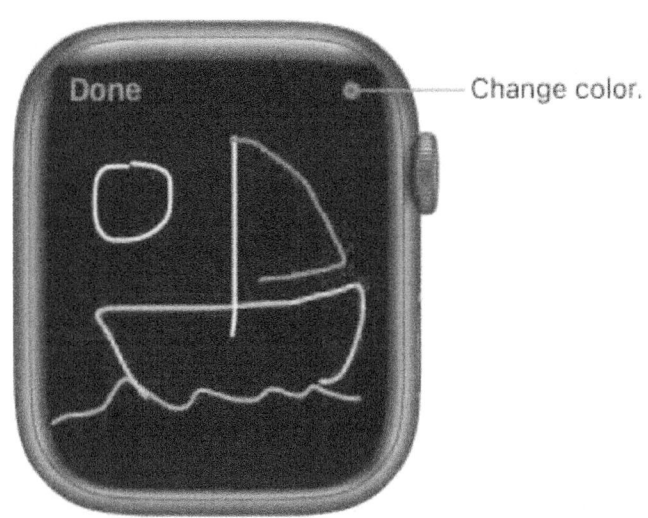

Done   •━━━━━━ Change color.

Digital Touch is a method to express your emotions.

Digital Touch allows you to send taps, a kiss, or your heartbeat to companions with an Apple Watch or iPhone running iOS 10 or later.

To receive a tap or pulse from someone, tap the notification.

1. compose a message, then touch.

2. Tap the canvas to access it, then use gestures to send the following:

- Tap: Tap the screen once to transmit a single tap or tap multiple times to send a tap pattern.

- Kiss: Tap the display with two fingers once or more, but do not tap again to send.

- Heartbeat: Touch the screen with two fingertips until you can feel and see your heartbeat on the display.

- Heartbreak: Place two fingers on the display until you feel your pulse, and then drag them downwards to send.

- Fireball: Touch and hold the screen with one finger until a flame appears, then release to send.

Give individuals your location

Scroll down and then tap transmit Location to transmit a map of your current location to someone.

Ensure Share My Location is enabled in Settings⚙ > [your name] > Find My > Share My Location on your paired iPhone. Alternatively, open the Settings app on your Apple Watch with cellular and navigate to Privacy > Location Services before enabling Share My Location.

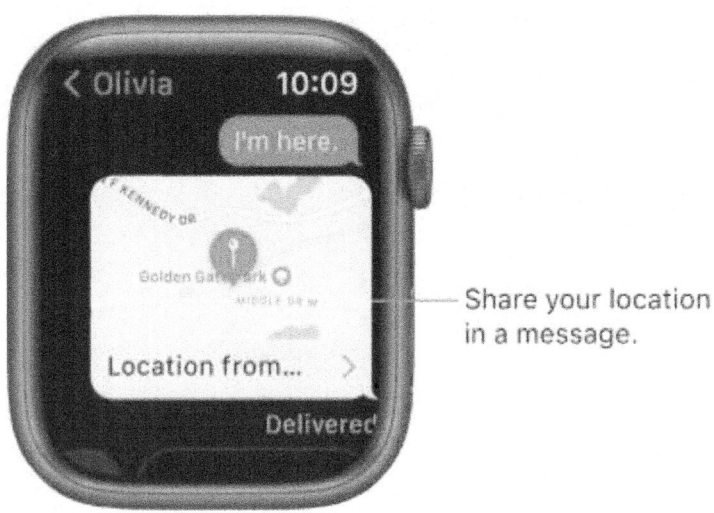

Share your location in a message.

Make contact with the recipient of your message.

While viewing a conversation, scroll downwards.

2.Choose Details, then select 📞 , 💬 , ✉ , or 📷 .

Scroll down and select "Share Contact" to share the contact with others.

Apple Watch permits you to reply to text messages.

To respond to a communication

Turn the Digital Crown to read the message's entirety, and then decide how to respond.

Touch and hold a specific message in a conversation, then select a Tapback such as a thumbs-up or a heart to swiftly respond with a Tapback.

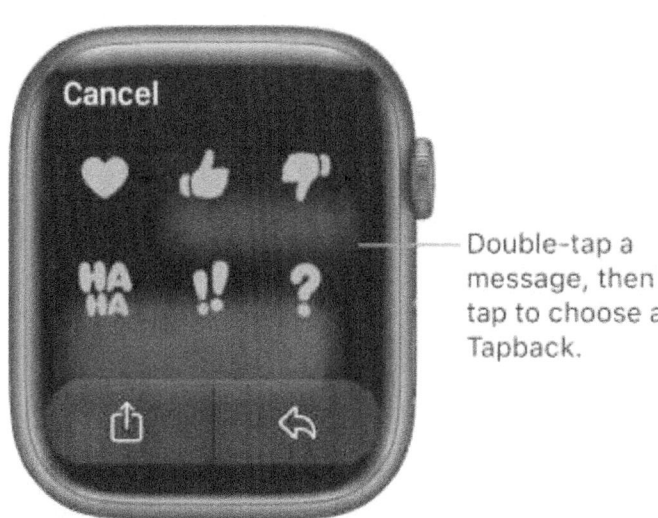

Double-tap a message, then tap to choose a Tapback.

You can respond directly to a single message in a conversation.

In a group conversation, you can reply to a specific message inline to help keep things organized.

1. Touch and hold the message you wish to reply to in a conversation in Messages, then touch ↰.

2. Enter your response and then select Send.

The message is read only by the recipient of your reply.

Transmit a communication

Messages from friends frequently contain information and emotions that you wish to share with others. To share a message, follow these steps:

1. Touch and hold a message within a Conversation in Messages, then touch $\square$.

2. Select the contacts with whom you correspond most frequently or tap Messages or Mail.

3. If you selected Messages or Mail, add contacts and a subject if you're sending an email.

4. Select Send.

Chapter 12

Add music to Apple Watch

When you add music to your Apple Watch, you can listen to it anywhere, even if your iPhone is not nearby.

You can add specific playlists and albums to your Apple Watch via the Apple Watch app on your iPhone. If you are an Apple Music subscriber, you can also upload music to your Apple Watch using the Music app .

If you have an Apple Music subscription, you do not need to choose specific recordings to add to your Apple Watch. Recent music you have listened to is automatically appended. (If you haven't listened to anything, Apple Music will add music it believes you'll enjoy.)

You can add music purchased through Apple Music Voice to your Apple Watch. If you wish to add songs, albums, and playlists from Apple Music, you must subscribe to Apple Music in its entirety.

Utilize your iPhone to upload songs.

1. On your iPhone, launch the Apple Watch application.
2. Click My Watch, followed by Music.
3. Select Add Music beneath Playlists & Albums.
4. Select albums and playlists for synchronization with your Apple Watch.

When your iPhone is nearby and connected into your Apple Watch, music is added.

Tip: Utilize the Music app on your iPhone to create compilations of music for your Apple Watch. For instance, you could create a workout-inspireddelta playlist.

The Apple Watch can be used to upload music.

If you have Apple Music, you can add music to your Apple Watch.

The Apple Music Voice Plan does not permit the addition of music.

1. On your Apple Watch, launch the Music application .
2. Select "Listen Now" or "Search," and then locate the desired music.

3. Tap an album or playlist, then tap and then press Add to Library.

A notice indicates that the item was added.

Note: If you have an internet connection, your Apple Watch can transmit music you've downloaded to it. You must acquire music before you can listen to it when you are not connected to the Internet.

4. select once more, then select Download to save the song to your Apple Watch.

Music is added when the Apple Watch is connected to power and Wi-Fi.

Apple Watch now permits the addition of a workout playlist.

You can add a playlist from your music library to the Workout app on Apple Watch, which will play automatically when you begin a workout.

1. On your iPhone, launch the Apple Watch application.
2. Select My Watch, followed by Workout.
3. Select a workout playlist via the Workout Playlist menu.

The playlist is added to the My Watch > Music > Playlists section of the Apple Watch app on the iPhone.

A workout playlist will not play if you are currently listening to music or audio.

Remove songs from your Apple Watch.

If you're running out of space to store music on your Apple Watch, you may need to delete automatically added music or music you no longer listen to.

Open the Settings app on your Apple Watch and navigate to General > Storage to view the amount of music on your device. Additionally, you can open the Apple Watch application on your iPhone, select My Watch, and then navigate to General > Storage.

You can delete songs from your iPhone.

1. On your iPhone, launch the Apple Watch application.

2. Tap My Watch, tap Music, and then select one of the subsequent options:

- To get rid of music you've already added, tap Edit and then touch ⊖ the items you want to get rid of.

- If music was automatically added to your Apple Watch, disable Recent Music and any other automatically added music.

Note that recently played music will not be added to Apple Watch until Recent Music is once again enabled.

When you remove music from your Apple Watch, it remains on your iPhone.

Music can be deleted from your Apple Watch.

If you have Apple Music, you can remove music from your Apple Watch, regardless of whether it was added automatically or manually.

1. On your Apple Watch, launch the Music application 🎵.
2. Playlists or Albums can be accessed by selecting Library, scrolling down to Downloaded, and then selecting Playlists or Albums.
3. Swipe to the left on a playlist or album, touch, and then tap Remove to remove it.
4. Touch Delete.

Your Apple Watch and all other devices using the same Apple ID will no longer play music.

You can also remove a single song at a time. If you swipe left on a song, tap ⋯, touch Remove, and then tap Delete, the song will be deleted from your Apple Watch and all other devices using the same Apple ID.

Apple Watch can play music.

Utilize the Apple Watch Music app to select and play music. You can play stored music on Apple Watch, control audio on your iPhone, and stream music from Apple Music and Apple audio Voice with a subscription.

Apple Music Voice Plan does not include all features.

Say something similar to

- "Play the song "Enough for You" by Olivia Rodrigo,"
- "Play more songs from this album,"
- "Play my workout music playlist,"
- "Play Apple Music Country,"
- "Play cool jazz,"
- "Play the dinner party's music playlist,"
- "Play me a playlist to help me relax," or
- "Play more like this."

Create music

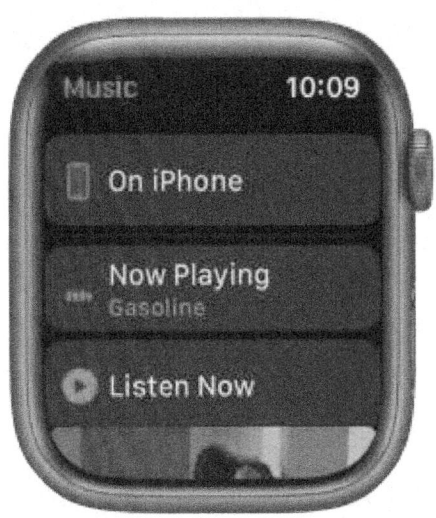

Open the Music app on your Apple Watch after pairing it with Bluetooth headphones or speakers.

- Turn the Digital Crown to view the album art, then select a playlist or album to play it.
  Using the Apple Watch app on your iPhone, you can choose which music to store on Apple Watch.
- To play music from your iPhone without using Bluetooth, tap On iPhone at the top of the screen, then press a playlist, artist, or song to play it.
- To listen to music from your music library, select Library and then a playlist, artist, album, or song. To play downloaded music on your Apple Watch, select Downloaded and then Music.
- Ask Apple Music for music (you need an Apple Music or Apple Music Voice subscription): Raise your wrist and then ask for an artist, album, song, genre, or portion of a song's lyrics.

Play some music for you.

If you have Apple Music, you can listen to specially curated music.

1. On your Apple Watch, launch the Music application 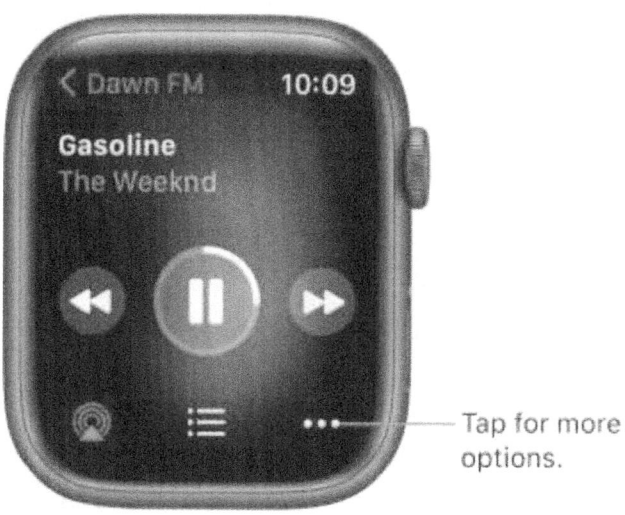.

2. Scroll to the top of the screen and select Listen Now to view a feed of playlists and albums curated for you based on what you like and dislike.

3. Touch a category, followed by an album or playlist, and finally ▶ .

Tap for more options.

Start the queue

When playing music, you can see what songs are next in the backlog.

1. On your Apple Watch, launch the Music application .

2. Tap ≣ to play an album or list of tracks.

3. Tap a track in the queue to listen to it.

Auto Play assigns similar music to the end of the queue by default.

To stop Auto Play from playing, tap ∞ the icon.

Note: When you disable Auto Play on a device that uses your Apple ID, such as your Apple Watch, it ceases functioning only on that device. Auto Play will continue to function on other devices until you disable it individually.

To add an item to the queue, swipe left on a song, playlist, or album, tap • • • , and then touch Play Next or Play Last. The music you wish to hear last is placed last in the order.

Change the song playing

To adjust the volume, simply rotate the Digital Crown. Here's how to listen to music on an iPhone or Apple Watch:

▶ Play the current song.

‖ Pause playback.

▶▶ Skip to the next song.

◀◀ Skip to the beginning of the song; double-tap to skip to the previous song.

Alternate or repeat the audio.

- You can shuffle albums, songs, and artists on the Music interface by tapping an album, artist, or playlist and then tapping .

- Tap ⬚ and then tap ⤭ or ↻ while on the playback screen to shuffle or repeat music.

Tap Repeat twice to play a tune twice.

Music on Apple Watch expands your capabilities.

You can inform Music what you like, add songs to the library, and perform other actions.

On Apple Watch, you can add music to your library, remove songs, indicate what you like and dislike, add songs to the queue, browse an artist's discography, and view albums and playlists. Any of the following:

- Review your options on the "Now Playing" screen; tap ⋯ and select an option while the music is playing.

- Look at the Listen Now and Library options: Swipe left on a song, playlist, or album, hit••• , and then choose an option. To add the item to your collection, tap + it.

Apple Music Voice Plan does not include all features.

Share music

You can share playlists, albums, and songs with Apple Music.

1. On your Apple Watch, launch the Music application 🎵.
2. Touch iPhone, Now Playing, or Library.
3. Choose from Playlists, Albums, and Songs.
4. Swipe left on a playlist, album, or single, then tap••• followed by Share [Playlist, Album, single].
5. Choose a mode of sharing.

To share a song, tap••• the Now Playing interface and then select Share Song. If you're listening to a tune on a radio station, you can also select Share Station.

Choose the cellular connection settings.

To listen to music over cellular, you must have an Apple Watch with cellular.

1. On your iPhone, navigate to Settings > Music and then enable Cellular Data.
2. Choose a quality by selecting Audio Quality, Cellular Streaming, and then a quality.

Note: Quality settings consume significantly more data.

Apple Watch is capable of playing radio.

Apple Music , Apple Music Hits, and Apple Music Country reside in the Radio section of the Music app on Apple Watch. These three Apple Music stations feature the newest music from a variety of genres, as well as interviews with the artists. Additionally, you can listen to live radio and featured stations created by music experts.

Apple Music, Apple Music Hits, and Apple Music Country are all free to listen to.

Apple Music radio is audible.

To listen to Apple Music radio, your Apple Watch must be near to your iPhone or connected to a Wi-Fi network — or a cellular network, if your Apple Watch supports cellular.

1. On your Apple Watch, launch the Music application.

2. Select Radio followed by Apple Music 1, Apple Music Hits, or Apple Music Country.

Listen to a featured or genre-specific station.

1. On your Apple Watch, launch the Music application .
2. Tap Radio, then turn the Digital Crown to navigate through music-expert-curated stations and genres.
3. Touch a genre to display its stations, then touch a station to begin playing it.

Listen to the radio

You can listen to thousands of broadcast radio stations on your Apple Watch.

Siri: Say phrases such as "Play Wild 94.9" and "Tune in to ESPN Radio."

You can request stations by their name, call sign, frequency, or alias.

Note: An Apple Music subscription is not required to listen to broadcast radio. Not all nations or regions have access to broadcast radio. Not all stations are audible in all nations or regions.

Choose a photo album and manage Apple Watch storage

With the photographs app 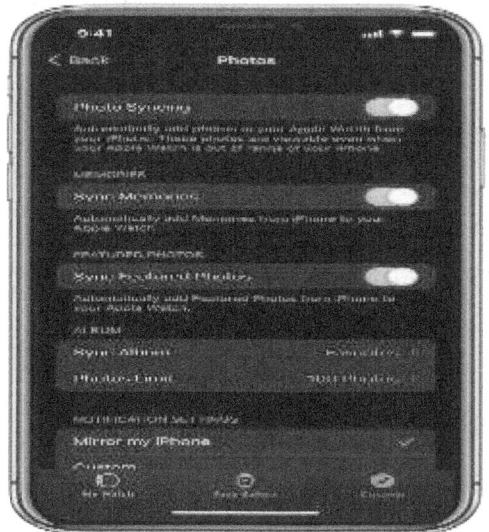 on your Apple Watch, you can view photographs from the album of your choosing on your iPhone, in addition to featured photos and Memories.

Choose the album to add to your Apple Watch.

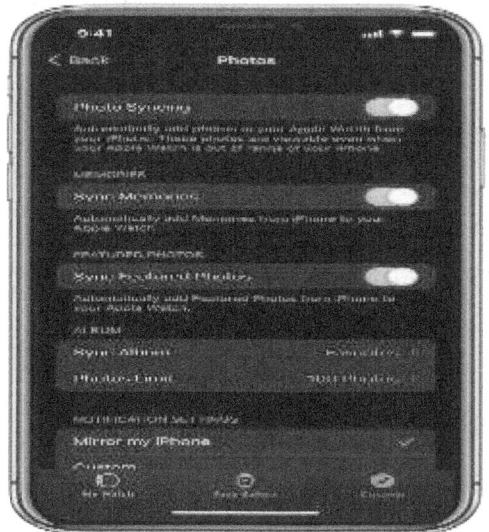

When you first receive an Apple Watch, it is configured to display photos from your Favorites album. However, you can change which album it utilizes.

1. On your iPhone, launch the Apple Watch application.
2. Tap "My Watch," then "Photos," then "Sync Album," followed by the album's name.

To remove a photo from Apple Watch, launch the Photos app on your iPhone and then delete the image from the synced album.

Create a new album on your iPhone's Photos program for your Apple Watch photos.

Photos and Memories can be viewed on the Apple Watch.

Your Apple Watch can automatically integrate with the photo library on your iPhone to obtain featured photos and Memories.

1. On your iPhone, launch the Apple Watch application.
2. My Watch > Photos > Sync Memories and Sync Featured Photos.

Stop synchronizing your photographs

If you don't want your iPhone to sync your Memories, featured photos, or photographs from a specific album, take the following steps:

1. On your iPhone, launch the Apple Watch application.
2. To disable photo synchronization, navigate to "My Watch," tap "Photos," and then press "Photo Syncing"

Apple Watch has a limited capacity for photos.

How many photos you can store on your Apple Watch depends on the available storage space. You can restrict the number of photos stored on the device so that you have more space for recordings and other content.

1. On your iPhone, launch the Apple Watch application.
2. Select "My Watch," "Photos," and "Photos Limit."

Choose one of the following to determine the number of photos on your Apple Watch:

- Launch the Settings program ⚙ on your Apple Watch and navigate to General > About.

- Launch the Apple Watch app on your iPhone, select "My Watch," and then navigate to "General" > "About."

Open the Settings app ⚙ on your Apple Watch and go to General > Storage to see how much space your photos are taking up. Launch the Apple Watch application on your iPhone, select My Watch, and then navigate to General > Storage.

Get a picture of Apple Watch.

1. Launch the Settings program ⚙ on your Apple Watch and navigate to General > Screenshots. Then, activate the Screenshots option.

2. To capture an image of the screen, simultaneously press the Digital Crown and the side button.

iPhone screenshots are stored in the Photos app.

A Apple Watch can display photos and memories.

On Apple Watch, you can use the Photos app to look through your photos and choose one to display on your watch face.

Tap to view a photo.

Use the Photos app on Apple Watch to view images.

Follow the steps below after launching the Photos app on your Apple Watch to browse through your photos.

1. Tap a memory, Featured Photos, or a synced album on your Apple Watch.

2. Touch an image to view it.

3. Swipe left or right to view additional images.

- Rotate the Digital Crown to magnify in or out, or drag it to navigate within an image.

- Zoom out as much as possible to view the entire photo album.

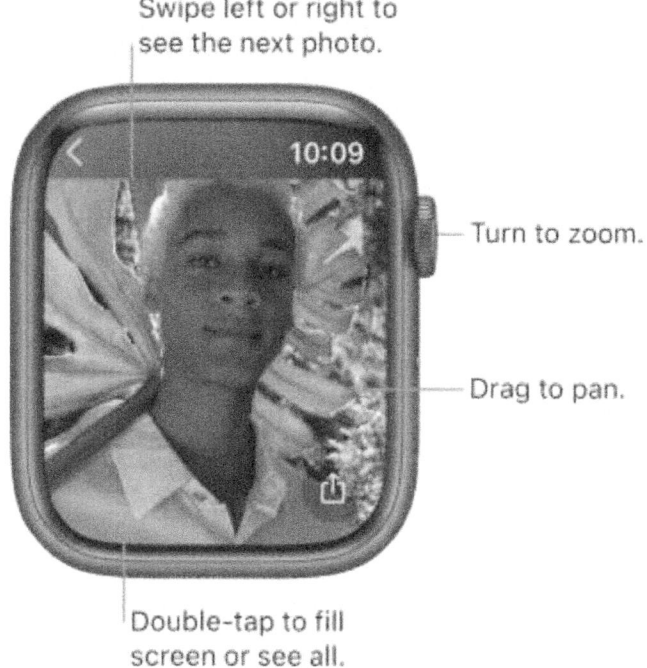

Swipe left or right to see the next photo.

Turn to zoom.

Drag to pan.

Double-tap to fill screen or see all.

Look at a memory on the face of the watch

Memories can be viewed on the Apple Watch in the Photos app and on the Siri and Photos watch faces.

- The Siri watch face provides access to recent memories. Select the Siri watch face and then select a memory to accomplish this.

- You can view photos from Memories on the Photos watch face by opening the Apple Watch app on your iPhone, tapping Face Gallery, tapping the Photos watch face, and then tapping Dynamic.

The Dynamic watch face displays images from your most recent Memories, with new images being added as they are created.

Apple Watch permits viewing of a Live Photo.

Touch and hold the Live Photo icon in the bottom-left quadrant of a photo.

Post an image

When viewing a photo in the Photos app on your Apple Watch, you can tap and select a sharing method.

Create a watch face from a photograph

While viewing a photograph in the Photos app on your Apple Watch, tap , scroll down, and then touch Create Face. You can also use the image to create a Kaleidoscope or Photos watch face in the Apple Watch app on your iPhone.

Creating a watch face on an iPhone is simple. Launch the Photos application on your iPhone, tap a photo, touch, swipe up, tap Create Watch Face, and then select between Portraits, Photos, and Kaleidoscope.

Apple Watch allows you to set and manage reminders.

When a reminder is set in the Reminders app on your Apple Watch, iPhone, or any other iOS device, iPad, or Mac where your Apple ID is signed in, your Apple Watch will notify you.

View your remembrances

1. Launch the Reminders app on your Apple Watch.
2. Tap a list to access it.

3. Tap the item's left edge to label it as completed, or tap

    ◯ the reminder and then tap label as Completed.

4. To return to the list view, tap the in the upper-left quadrant.

5. Tap the list, tap View Options, and then tap Show Completed to view completed reminders.

Tap the All list, tap View Options, and then tap Show Completed to display all completed reminders.

To change the order of your lists, open the Reminders app on your iPhone, select Edit, and then drag the list to a new location.

People who use iCloud can collaborate on a shared inventory. Shared profiles allow you to determine who an alert is for. You can join a shared list from your Apple Watch, but you cannot create a shared list.

Turn to see more lists.

Tap to view the items.

Respond to a reminder notification

• Tap the notification, swipe (or turn the Digital Crown to navigate) the reminder, and then tap Mark as Completed or select a time to be reminded.

- If you discover the notification later, select it in your list of notifications, scroll, and then respond.

Establish a reminder

- Use Siri by saying, "Remind me to pick up my dry cleaning at 5 o'clock."
- Siri on Apple Watch can also be used to create a schedule.
- Use the Reminders app to schedule a reminder: Scroll to the bottom of any list, and then tap "Add Reminder."

Delete a reminder.

1. Launch the Reminders app on your Apple Watch.
2. Tap a list to access it, and then perform one of the subsequent actions:

- Swipe the notification to the left, and then tap.

Tap the reminder, scroll down, then tap the Delete button.

Change a reminder

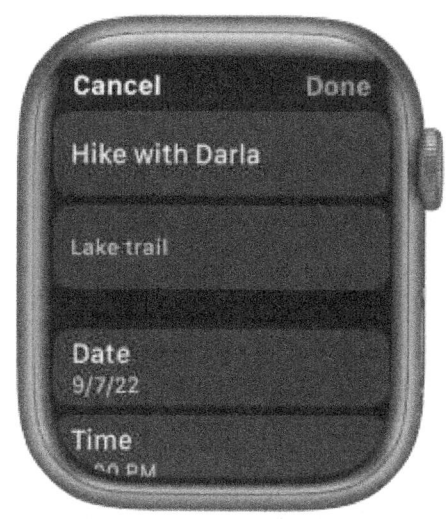

You can administer and alter reminders on an Apple Watch that you've configured for yourself.

1. Launch the Reminders app on your Apple Watch.
2. press a list, press a reminder, tap Edit, and then perform any of the subsequent actions:

- Rename the reminder: Touch the reminder's name, then enter a new name using the QWERTY and QuickPath keyboard (not available in all languages, only on Apple Watch Series 7 and Apple Watch Series 8), dictation, Scribble, or emoji.
- Please note that Scribble is not supported in all languages.
- To add a note, tap Add Notes and then enter the text for the note.
- Add a date and time by selecting Date from the Date menu. Tap Time, then AM or PM, then the hours or minutes, and then revolve the Digital Crown to select a time.

- touch Tags, and then touch an existing tag or Create New to create a new one.

- Add a location: Tap Location, then choose where you'd like to be reminded, such as when you enter your home or a vehicle that can connect to your Apple Watch via Bluetooth.

- Flag serves as a reminder: Activate Flag.

- Select a priority by touching Priority followed by Low, Medium, or High.

- Transfer the reminder to a different list by selecting List and then a list.

Apple Watch can monitor your sleep patterns.

With the Sleep app on Apple Watch, you can set bedtime schedules that will help you achieve your sleep objectives. If you wear your Apple Watch to bed, it can approximate the length of time you spent in REM, Core, and Deep sleep, as well as when you awoke. When you wake up, open the Sleep app to view your sleep duration and how it has changed over the past 14 days.

If your Apple Watch has less than 30 percent charge before slumber, you will be prompted to recharge it. Simply glance at the wake-up message to determine how much charge remains.

You can create multiple schedules, such as one for weekdays and one for weekends. You may configure the following for each schedule:

- A slumber objective (number of hours of sleep desired).
- When you would like to go to sleep and rise up
- An alarm to jolt you awake
- When to activate Sleep Focus, which reduces distractions before bedtime and safeguards your sleep once you're in bed.
- Sleep tracking, which utilizes your motion to detect sleep when Apple Watch is worn to bed and Sleep Focus is activated

To deactivate Sleep Focus, press and hold the Digital Crown. Swipe upwards to access the Control Center, and then tap.

Apple Watch sleep mode

1. Open the Sleep application on the Apple Watch.

2. Follow the instructions on screen.

You can also launch the Health app on an iPhone, tap Browse, tap Sleep, and then tap Get Started (under Set Up Sleep).

Change or disable your next alarm schedule

1. Open the Sleep application on the Apple Watch.
2. Tap the current time of your bedtime.

Tap the wake-up time, rotate the Digital Crown to the desired time, and then tap .

If you do not want your Apple Watch to rouse you up in the morning, turn off Alarm.

You can also modify your schedule by launching the Health application on your iPhone, tapping Browse, tapping Sleep, and then tapping Edit below Your Schedule.

The modifications will only affect your next alarm clock. Following that, everything will return to normal.

Note: In the Alarms app, you can also disable the upcoming wake-up alarm. Simply select the alarm that appears under Sleep |

Wake Up , followed by Skipping Tonight.

Change or add a sleep time

1. Open the Sleep application on the Apple Watch.
2. Tap Full Schedule, then select one of the options below:
- Tap the existing schedule to modify a sleep schedule.
- To create a sleep schedule, tap the "Add Schedule" button.
- Modify your sleep goal: Tap Sleep Goal and then enter the desired amount of sleep time.
- Modify the amount of time it takes to wound down: Tap wound Down, then select the amount of time you want Sleep Focus to be active before bed.
Sleep Focus powers off your watch's display and activates Do Not Disturb just before bedtime.
3. Choose one of the following:
- Select the days you wish to work by tapping your calendar and then tapping Active On. Select the desired days, then tap.
- Alter your wake-up and bedtime times by tapping your schedule, touching Wake Up or Bedtime, rotating the Digital

Crown to set a new time, and then tapping .

- Configure the alarm settings: select your schedule, then select Alarm to enable or disable the alarm. Tap Sound & Haptics in order to select an alarm sound.

Note: To delete or cancel a sleep schedule, tap your schedule, then touch Delete Schedule (at the bottom of the screen) to remove an existing schedule or Cancel (at the top of the screen) to cancel the creation of a new one.

Modify sleeping alternatives

1. On the Apple Watch, launch the Settings application.
2. Tap Sleep, then make the following adjustments:
- Activate when winding down: By default, Sleep Focus activates at the time specified in the Sleep app for winding down. Turn this option off if you'd rather use Control Center to manage Sleep Focus on your own.
- Sleep Screen: The Apple Watch display and iPhone lock screen have been simplified to be less distracting.
- Show Time: When Sleep Focus is enabled, your iPhone and Apple Watch will display the date and time.
3. Toggle Sleep Tracking and Reminders to Charge on or off.

When Sleep Tracking is activated, your Apple Watch monitors your sleep and sends the data to the Health app on your iPhone.

Enable Charging Reminders to have your Apple Watch remind you to charge it before bed and notify you when it is fully charged.

You can also modify these sleep parameters on your iPhone. Open the Apple Watch app on your iPhone, tap "My Watch," then touch "Sleep."

See how you slept previously.

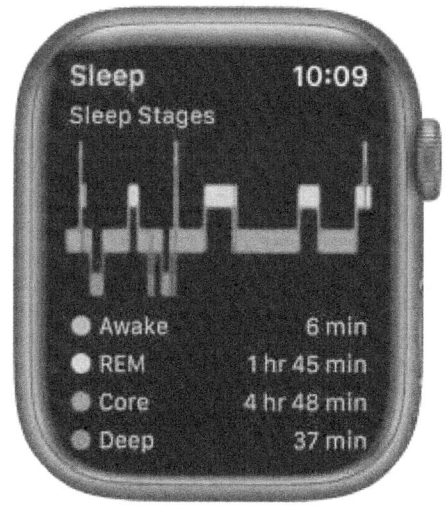

1. Open the Sleep application on the Apple Watch.
2. Scroll down to see how much sleep you received the night before, how long you spent in each sleep stage, and your average sleep over the last 14 days.

Open the Health app on your iPhone, hit Browse, and then tap Sleep to view your sleep history. To view additional information, such as how long you spent on average in each sleep stage, tap Show More Sleep Data.

Check your breathing rate during sleep.

Your Apple Watch can help you monitor your respiration rate while you sleep. This can provide more information about your overall health. After wearing your watch to bed, perform the following:

1. Open the Health app on your iPhone, select Browse, then tap Respiratory.

2. Select Respiratory Rate, then select Show Additional Respiratory Rate Data.

The range of your respiration rate during sleep is displayed in the Sleep entry.

Note that Respiratory Rate measurements are not intended for use in medicine.

Check the temperature of your wrist (Apple Watch Series 8 only).

Wear your Series 8 Apple Watch to bed to monitor how your wrist temperature fluctuates throughout the night. This can provide you with health-related information. Cycle Tracking can use information from your wrist temperature to more accurately determine your period and estimate when you ovulated in the past.

Wear your Apple Watch with Sleep Tracking activated to bed. This will provide a baseline temperature reading. After approximately five nights, wrist temperature data will be available.

1. Launch the Health application on your iPhone, then select Browse.

2. Select Body Measurements followed by Wrist Temperature.

3. Tap a point on the graph to view sample information.

Apple Watch allows you to monitor stock prices.

Using the stocks app 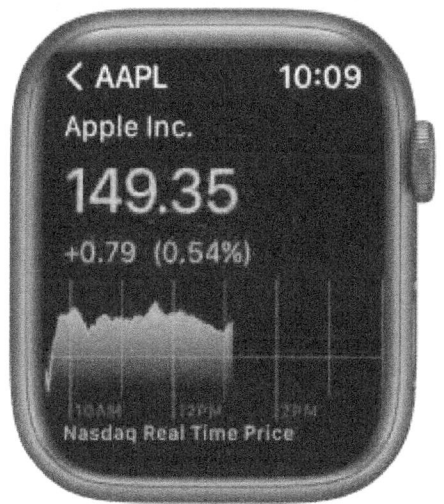 on your Apple Watch, you can receive information about the equities you follow on your iPhone.

< AAPL   10:09
Apple Inc.
149.35
+0.79 (0.54%)

Nasdaq Real Time Price

Siri can answer questions such as "What was the last price of Apple stock today?"

Add and subtract commodities

You can add and withdraw stocks directly from your Apple Watch using the Stocks app on your iPhone. Simply launch the Stocks application on your Apple Watch to:

- To add a stock, scroll to the bottom of the screen and select "Add Stock." Type the stock's name (only on Apple Watch Series 7 and Apple Watch Series 8), or use Scribble or dictation to enter it. Select the stock name from the list.
  To use Scribble on an Apple Watch Series 7 or Series 8, swipe up from the bottom of the display and then touch Scribble. Scribble is not supported in all languages.

- To sell a stock, swipe left on the stock you wish to sell and then press the X key.

To rearrange stocks on your Apple Watch, tap and hold a stock, then drag it to a new location.

Additionally, you can open the Stocks application on your iPhone, tap, touch Edit Watchlist, drag a stock to the desired location, and then tap Done.

When you change the order on one device, the other device follows likewise.

Check Apple Watch stock information.

1. Open the Stocks application on the Apple Watch.
2. Select an investment from the list.
3. Tap the upper-left corner to return to the list of securities, or turn the Digital Crown to advance to the next stock.

Choose the stock displayed on the Siri watch face.

1. On the Apple Watch, launch the Settings application .
2. Go to Stocks > Selected Stock and select a stock from the drop-down menu.

Select data indicators

You can select which data metrics appear in the Stocks app, Stocks complications, and Siri watch face. Follow the instructions below:

- Change the data metric in the Stocks app: On your Apple Watch, open the Stocks app, swipe down, touch Viewing, and then select Points, Market Capitalization, or Percentage.

- Modify the data metric for the Siri watch face and the Stocks complications by opening the Settings app on your Apple Watch, tapping Stocks, tapping Data Metric, and then selecting a metric.

Additionally, you can activate the Apple Watch application on your iPhone, tap My Watch, tap Stocks, and then select a metric.

Replace your iPhone with Stocks.

1. Open the Stocks application on the Apple Watch.
1. 2.Activate the iPhone's App Switcher. (On an iPhone with Face ID, swipe up and halt from the bottom edge; on an iPhone with a Home button, double-click the Home button.)
2. 3.To access Stocks, select the button at the bottom of the display.

On Apple Watch, you can time events using a stopwatch.

You can accurately and conveniently time occurrences. Apple Watch can time full events (up to 11 hours and 55 minutes) and monitor lap or split times, displaying the results in a list, graph, or on the watch face. Incorporated into the Chronograph and Chronograph Pro watch faces is a chronograph.

Open a chronometer and select a time.

1. Launch the Stopwatch application 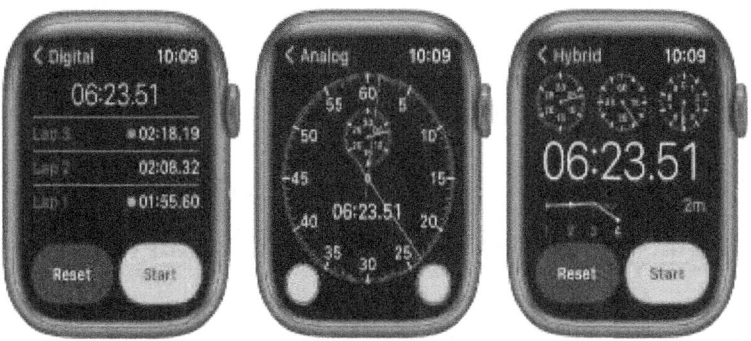 on your Apple Watch, or select the stopwatch icon on your watch face if you've added it or are using the Chronograph or Chronograph Pro watch face.

2. Select Analog, Digital, Graph, or Hybrid from the Stopwatch screen.

3. While gazing at a stopwatch, tap and then choose a different format.

Start, then pause, and reset the stopwatch.

Launch the Stopwatch application on your Apple Watch, select a format, and then perform any of the following:

- Press the "Start" button (the green button on the analog chronograph).
- Tap the circuit button (the white button on the analog stopwatch) to record a circuit.
- To record the final time, tap the Stop button (the red button on the analog stopwatch).
- Reset the timer to zero by pressing the Reset button (the white button on an analog stopwatch) when the timer stops.

Even if the watch face is changed or other apps are opened, the timer continues to run.

You can view the results on the display you used to time, or you can switch displays to view your lap times and fastest/slowest circuits (indicated by green and red) in a manner that is most convenient for you. If a catalog of lap times is displayed on the screen, rotate the Digital Crown to navigate the list.

Start or stop the stopwatch.

Record lap times.

Apple Watch permits setting of timers.

With the Timers app  on the Apple Watch, you can maintain track of time. You can configure up to 24 time-tracking devices.

Siri: "Set a timer for 20 minutes," for instance.

Set a timer quickly.

1. Open the Timers application on the Apple Watch.

2. To rapidly start a timer, tap a duration (such as 1, 3, or 5 minutes) or a timer you've recently used below Recents. Swipe down and then select Custom to create a personalized timer.

When a timer expires, you can tap  to initiate a new one with the same duration.

Stop or deactivate a timer

1. Open the Timers app while a timer is active on your Apple Watch.

2. Tap to start, tap to halt, and tap to start.

Create an individual timer

1. Open the Timers application on the Apple Watch.

2. Tap the Custom button at the top of the display.

3. Touch the hours, minutes, and seconds displays, then rotate the Digital Crown to make adjustments.

4. Press Start.

Tap hours, minutes, or seconds, then turn the Digital Crown.

Create numerous triggers

1. Open the Timers application on the Apple Watch.

2. Establish a timetable and activate it.

   Use Siri to set a timer if you'd like to name it "Pizza."

   Raise your Apple Watch and say, "Set a timer for pizza to

   be ready in 12 minutes."

3. Tap to return to the Timers screen, then create and initiate a new timer.

The Timers tab displays all active timers. touch **▌▌** a timer to pause it, and touch ▶ it again to restart it.

Swipe left and select X on the Timers screen to delete a running or paused timer.

You can mark a timer as a favorite

1. Open the Timers application ⏱ on the Apple Watch.

2. Swipe to the left on a recent timer, then touch ★ .

The timer is located under "Favorites."

Tips

In the Tips app ☀ , you can discover groups of tips that will help you use your Apple Watch better.

Get Advice

Using the Tips application ☀ on your Apple Watch, you can learn about new watchOS features, how to customize your watch, and much more.

How to use of an Apple Watch.

1. Open the Tips application  on the Apple Watch.

2. Tap a group of instructions, and then scroll down to view the individual tip.

    Tap  a tip with an animation to view it again.

3. If a tip has a button labeled "Try It," click it to see how it functions on your Apple Watch.

4. Move your finger to the left to view the next tip.

Apple Watch can record and replay audio memos.

Use the Voice Memos app on the Apple Watch to record personal notes.

Create a vocal note

1. Launch the Voice Memos application on the Apple Watch.

2. Tap .

3. To stop the recording, tap .

Perform a voice memo.

1. Launch the Voice Memos application on the Apple Watch.

2. touch a recording in Voice Memos, then touch ▶ again to play it.

3. To change the recording's name or eliminate it, tap ● ● ● , followed by Edit Name or eliminate.

Voice memos that you record on your Apple Watch sync automatically to your Mac, iPad, and other iOS devices where you have the same Apple ID signed in.

Use Walkie-Talkie on the Apple Watch

Walkie-Talkie is a simple and entertaining method to communicate with another Apple Watch user. Similar to an actual walkie-talkie, you press a button to speak and release it when you're ready to receive their response. Walkie-Talkie requires both participants to have connectivity via Bluetooth, Wi-Fi, or cell service.

Not all regions provide access to walkie-talkie.

Invite a companion to use Walkie-Talkie.

1. Open the Walkie-Talkie app  on your Apple Watch for the first time.

2. Scroll through the list of friends and tap a name to send an invitation.

If your contact accepts the request, you can start a Walkie-Talkie conversation whenever you are both free.

To add a second contact, tap "Add Friends" on the Walkie-Talkie's screen and then choose a contact.

Use a walkie-talkie to talk.

1. Launch the Walkie-Talkie application  on the Apple Watch.

2. Tap the name of the acquaintance.

3. Press and hold the Talk icon before speaking.

If your friend is available, Walkie-Talkie will open on their Apple Watch and they will hear what you say.

As you talk, turn the Digital Crown to change the volume setting.

Communicate with a single contact

If you find it difficult to maintain contact with the Talk button, you can speak with a single stroke.

1. On the Apple Watch, launch the Settings application.

2. Tap Accessibility, then activate Tap to Speak beneath Walkie-Talkie.

When this is enabled, you touch once to speak and again to end a conversation.

Alternatively, you can open the Apple Watch app on your iPhone, tap My Watch, select Accessibility, and then toggle Tap to Talk below Walkie-Talkie.

Get rid of contacts.

Swipe left on a contact in the Walkie-Talkie app on your Apple Watch, then select X.

Avoid making yourself available

1. 1.To access Control Center, tap and hold the bottom of the display, then swipe up.

2. Move downward and touch .

Or, navigate to the top of the Walkie-Talkie app on your Apple Watch to disable Walkie-Talkie.

When theater mode is enabled, Walkie-Talkie cannot be used.

Say something like, "What will the weather be like in Honolulu tomorrow?" and Siri will provide you with the information.

Check out the weather

- To view the weather and temperature for the day, launch the Weather app on your Apple Watch. Tap a place, then tap the screen to see hourly forecasts for rain, temperature, or weather.

Turn to see more weather information.

Tap to see temperature or precipitation forecast.

- Tap a place and drag the bottom bar to see the air quality, UV index, wind speed, humidity, visibility, and a 10-day forecast.

To return to the list of cities, tap the link in the upper-left corner.

Not everywhere has air quality monitoring capabilities.

Change how weather is measured

You can select a different metric to display below each city in the Weather app's list of cities.

1. Launch the Weather app 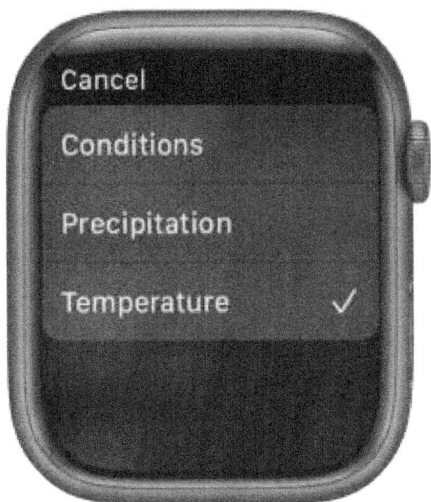 on your Apple Watch.

2. Select Viewing at the top of the display.

3. Select Weather, precipitation, or temperature.

Choose the city of your preference.

1. On the Apple Watch, launch the Settings application.

2. Select Weather, then Default City, followed by a city.

You can also use your iPhone to launch the Apple Watch app, navigate to Weather > Default City, and then select My Watch.

If you have added weather to the watch face, the city's weather is displayed.

Check the weather forecasts.

When a significant weather event is imminent, the Weather app may display an alert at the top.

Check the time in other locations with Apple Watch's World Clock.

Using the World Clock app  on your Apple Watch, you can determine the current time in cities throughout the globe.

What about "What time is it in Auckland?"?

World Clock permits the addition and removal of localities

1. Launch the World Clock app on your Apple Watch.
2. Click on "Add City."
3. Type the name of the city (only on Apple Watch Series 7 and Series 8), or input it using Scribble or dictation.
   To use Scribble, swipe up from the bottom of the screen and then touch it.
   Note: Scribble is not supported in all languages.

4. Tap the city's name to add it to the roster.

To remove a city from the list, swipe left on its name and then touch the X button.

The cities that you add to World Clock on your iPhone appear on your Apple Watch as well.

Find out what time it is in another city

1. Launch the World Clock app on your Apple Watch.
2. You can navigate the list by rotating the Digital Crown or scrolling the display.
3. Tap a city in the list to obtain additional information, such as sunrise and sunset times.
   While viewing information about a city, you can scroll to view the previous or following city in the list.
4. To return to the list of cities, tap the check mark in the upper left corner or swipe right.

You can add a World Clock to your watch face and select which city's time to display.

Turn to scroll through cities.

Change the way you call cities.

Follow these methods to modify an Apple Watch city abbreviation:

1. On your iPhone, launch the Apple Watch application.

2. Select "My Watch," then "Clock" and "City Abbreviations."

3. Touch any city to alter its textual form.

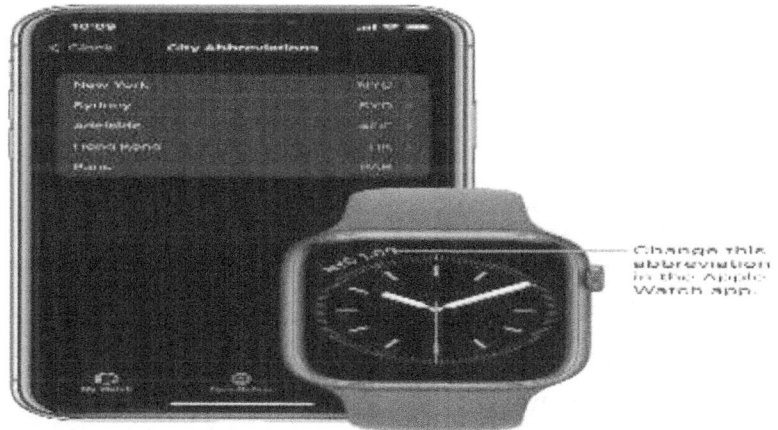

Change this abbreviation in the Apple Watch app.

VoiceOver support for Apple Watch

VoiceOver enables you to utilize your Apple Watch even if you cannot see the display. Use simple gestures to navigate the screen while VoiceOver reads aloud each selected item.

VoiceOver can be activated or Desactivated.

1. On the Apple Watch, launch the Settings application⚙️.
2. Click Accessibility followed by VoiceOver to enable VoiceOver.

Double-tap the VoiceOver icon to disable the feature.

Siri responds to "Turn on VoiceOver" and "Turn off VoiceOver."

Additionally, you can use your iPhone to activate VoiceOver on your Apple Watch. Launch the Apple Watch app on your iPhone, select My Watch, navigate to Accessibility, and then select VoiceOver. Alternatively, you can use the shortcut for convenience.

VoiceOver is used for configuration

VoiceOver can assist you in configuring your Apple Watch. You can accomplish this during setup by selecting the Digital Crown three times.

VoiceOver motions

VoiceOver enables you to control your Apple Watch with the gestures listed below.

The Always On Display is compatible with VoiceOver. When you tap the dimmed display, VoiceOver zeroes in on the object you contacted.

*   Explore the entire screen. Move your finger around the screen, and the name of each object you touch will be spoken aloud. You can also touch an item to select it or swipe

279

left or right with one finger to select the item next to the selected item. To view other pages, swipe left, right, up, or down with two fingers.

- To return to the previous screen, use two fingertips to form a "z" on the screen if you unexpectedly followed a path.

- Act on an item: When VoiceOver is enabled, use a double tap rather than a single tap to open an application, change an option, or perform any other action that would typically be performed with a tap. You can double-tap an app icon, list item, or option transition after tapping or swiping to it. To disable VoiceOver, for example, you would double-tap anywhere on the screen after tapping the VoiceOver icon.

- Perform additional functions: some items allow you to perform additional functions. When selecting an item, listen for the phrase "actions available." Swipe up or down to select an action, then double-tap to execute it.

- To halt VoiceOver from reading, use two fingers to tap the screen. To return, press with two fingers again.

- Adjust VoiceOver volume: Double-tap with two fingers and hold, then slide up or down. Alternatively, on your iPhone, launch the Apple Watch app, select My Watch, navigate to Accessibility > VoiceOver, and adjust the slider.

Use the rotor for VoiceOver

Using the rotor, you can alter VoiceOver settings and navigate between items on the screen. You can select Words, Characters,

Actions, Headings, Volume, and Speaking Rate using the rotor on Apple Watch.

When VoiceOver is enabled, move two fingertips across the screen as if turning a dial. VoiceOver describes how to configure the rotor. Turn your fingers to hear additional parameters. When the desired setting is audible, cease moving your fingers.

Utilize the rotor as described.

Action	Gesture
Choose a rotor setting	Rotate two fingers
Move to the previous item or increase (depending on the rotor setting)	Swipe up
Move to the next item or decrease (depending on the rotor setting)	Swipe down

Adjust VoiceOver settings

From your Apple Watch, you can modify VoiceOver's behavior. Launch the Settings application on your Apple Watch, navigate to Accessibility > VoiceOver, and then take any of the following actions:

Stop employing VoiceOver.

- Alter your velocity of speech
- Adjust the VoiceOver volume
- Configure options for pronunciation

- Tap Speech and then select the desired voice, intonation, and rotor languages.
- Turn on or off haptics
- Set up the Braille choices.
- Tap Braille to choose choices for Braille output, Braille input, word wrap, the length of time an alert is shown, and Braille tables.
- Change the settings for the keyboard on the Apple Watch Series 7 and Apple Watch Series 8.
- Connect a Bluetooth keyboard to the Apple Watch, choose Keyboards, and then set up the phonetic feedback, typing feedback, control keys, keyboard interaction time, and devices.
- Turn off ideas from VoiceOver. Use the Digital Crown to find your way.
- When using VoiceOver, you have the option to hear the highlighted item's name when you elevate your wrist. You can also enable Screen Curtain, which disables the display for privacy.
- Discuss for seconds
- Establish hand motions

You can accomplish all of these on your iPhone. Launch the Apple Watch application, select My Watch, then navigate to Accessibility > VoiceOver.

Apple Watch can be set up by using VoiceOver.

VoiceOver can help you pair your Apple Watch with your iPhone and set it up. To turn on VoiceOver, touch and hold the screen, then move your finger around the screen or swipe left or right. Double-tap the thing that is highlighted to turn it on.

VoiceOver can be utilized to configure Apple Watch.

1. If your Apple Watch is not on, press and hold the side button (below the Digital Crown) until it is.

2. Triple-click the Digital Crown to activate VoiceOver on your Apple Watch.

3. Position your iPhone near your Apple Watch.

4. On your iPhone, select Continue followed by Continue twice.

5. Double-tap the Set Up Apple Watch option on the iPhone.

6. Try automatic synchronization by pointing the iPhone camera at the watch from about 6 inches away.
   Follow the verbal instructions when the coupling confirmation is audible. You can try pairing manually by following steps 7 through 13 if you're having difficulty.

7. Select Manually Pair Apple Watch on your iPhone, then double-tap.

8. Tap the Info icon twice in the bottom right corner of your Apple Watch.

9. Select your Apple Watch ID near the top of your Apple Watch's display. You hear the unique identifier for your Apple Watch, which sounds like "Apple Watch 52345"

10. Double-tap the corresponding icon on your iPhone.

11. Choose the six-digit synchronization code on the Apple Watch to hear it.

12. Utilize the iPhone's keyboard to enter the code from your Apple Watch.

    If pairing is successful, Apple Watch taps your wrist and announces, "Your Apple Watch is paired." If pairing fails, tap to respond to the notifications. After resetting your Apple Watch and the Apple Watch app on your iPhone, you can try again.

13. On your iPhone, select Restore from Backup or Set Up as New Apple Watch, and then double-tap.

14. Listen to the voice prompts to continue setting up your Apple Watch.

    After Apple Watch is configured, it connects to your iPhone. This will require some time. On your iPhone, tap Sync Progress to hear how far along it is. When you hear "sync complete," your Apple Watch is operational and displays the watch face. Swipe left or right to view the watch face's features.

Chapter 13

Apple Watch basics with VoiceOver

VoiceOver enables you to perform a variety of tasks with your Apple Watch by pressing, scrolling, or rotating the Digital Crown. If the current watch face is visible, attempt the following.

- To alter the watch face, swipe left or right with two fingertips.

- To modify the appearance of a watch face, triple-tap the display, glide down to the Edit option, and double-tap. Use two fingers to swipe left or right to view the customizable features. Turn the Digital Crown to make adjustments to the selected feature. To save your modifications, press the Digital Crown and double-tap the face when you're finished.

- To view notifications, swipe down with two fingers on the watch face.

- You can access your notifications from the majority of other displays by tapping the time in the upper right corner of the screen and then swiping down with two fingers.

- Swipe up from the watch face with two fingertips to access the Control Center.

- Tap the clock in the upper-right corner of the display, and then swipe up with two fingertips. This opens the Control Center from the majority of other displays.

- To access the Dock, press the side button and then use the Digital Crown to navigate through your favorite applications, press the side button. Double-tapping an app will launch it.

- Open any app in Grid View: To access the Home Screen, press the Digital Crown once. Swipe left or right, tap, or drag your finger to select an app, then double-tap it to launch it. Or, you can use Siri to activate the app: hold down the Digital Crown until you feel a double tap, and then say "launch" followed by the app's name (for example, "launch Mail").

- To navigate to the Home Screen, press the Digital Crown once. Swipe to locate the Mail application, and double-tap it. Siri can also be activated by holding down the Digital Crown and saying "launch Mail" Turn the Digital Crown to navigate through the messages when the Mail app opens, and double-tap a message to read it. Utilize the Digital Crown to navigate the message.

- Utilize the Digital Crown to navigate. Triple-tap with two fingertips and then turn the Digital Crown to select an item. To deactivate Digital Crown Navigation, three double-taps are required.

Use your iPhone to operate Apple Watch.

People who have difficulty moving or moving their bodies may find it easier to operate their Apple Watch using the larger screen on their iPhone. Apple Watch Mirroring enables users to control Apple Watch using iPhone's assistant features, such as Voice Control and Switch Control. In lieu of touching the Apple Watch display, they can also use voice commands, auditory actions, head tracking, or external Made for iPhone switches.

The Apple Watch Series 6, Series 7, and Series 8 all support Apple Watch Mirroring.

1. Launch the Settings application on the paired iPhone.
2. To activate, navigate to Accessibility and then Apple Watch Mirroring.

    The display on your iPhone resembles the display on your Apple Watch. Utilize hand gestures on the image in the mirror.

- Scroll: Drag your finger up or down the screen.
- To navigate between displays, swipe the screen left or right.
- Tap the Digital Crown: Touch the Digital Crown icon on the display.
- Tap the on-screen icon to activate it.
- To use Siri, touch and hold the Digital Crown to the display.

Your Apple Watch can remotely control nearby devices.

You can control your Apple Watch with your iPhone, but you can also control your iPhone or iPad with your Apple Watch.

1. Launch the Apple Watch Settings application.
2. Go to Accessibility > Nearby Devices.

    Your iPhone or iPad must be on the same network and have the same Apple ID signed in to iCloud.

3. If multiple devices are nearby, select one by tapping a button.

Buttons resemble device controls and include the following:

- Tap "Home"
- Alter Apps
- Center for warnings
- Command Center
- Siri
- Choices (including media play controls and programmable hand gestures)

When VoiceOver is on your Apple Watch and you use it to control a nearby device, VoiceOver is also on the device you're controlling, and the VoiceOver gestures you use on your Apple Watch are performed on the device.

When Switch Control is enabled on a nearby device, the same controls (such as Move, Next, and Select) will appear on your watch.

AssistiveTouch is compatible with Apple Watch.

AssistiveTouch makes Apple Watch simpler to use for individuals who cannot touch the screen or press the buttons. You can use Apple Watch's built-in sensors to answer calls, manipulate an on-screen pointer, and access a menu of actions with hand gestures.

Using gestures, you can accomplish the following and more with AssistiveTouch:

- Tap the display

- Press and rotate the Digital Crown.

- Swipe between displays

- Hold the side button down

- Navigate to the Dock, Notification Center, and Center for Contextual Notifications.

- Exhibit programs

- Utilize Apple Pay

- Ensure the side button has been depressed twice

- Engage Siri

- Execute Siri's shortcut

HelpfulTouch must be established.

1. Launch the Apple Watch Settings application.

2. To enable AssistiveTouch, navigate to Accessibility > AssistiveTouch.

3. Tap Hand Gestures, and then ensure that Hand Gestures is enabled.

Tip: To learn how to use hand gestures, tap "Learn more" below the Hand Gestures toggle and then touch each gesture individually. When you tap a gesture, an animation demonstrates how to perform it correctly and how to enhance your performance.

Additionally, you can launch the Apple Watch app on your iPhone, tap My Watch, navigate to Accessibility > AssistiveTouch, and enable AssistiveTouch.

AssistiveTouch is compatible with Apple Watch.

With AssistiveTouch and Hand Gestures enabled, you can control your Apple Watch with the following gestures:

- Squeeze: Forward
- Return and forth:
- Tap: Crush
- Double-tapping: Display the Action Menu

To use AssistiveTouch with the Weather app while the Meridian watch face is displayed, for instance:

1. To activate AssistiveTouch, grasp the device twice.
   The Calendar complication is surrounded by a highlight.
2. To locate the Temperature problem, pinch and then compress.
3. When you launch the Weather app, you can switch between temperature and weather conditions with a single tap.
4. To view the Air Quality section, pinch once, and then press again to view the UV Index.
5. Tap twice to return to the Air Quality page.
6. When you double-press the touchscreen, the Action Menu will appear.
   Double-pinch the screen to proceed through the actions in reverse.
7. Select the action "Press Crown," then compress the crown once to return to the watch face.

Use the Pointer to Move

You may manage your Apple Watch with the Motion Pointer by angling it up and down and side to side in addition to pinching and squeezing. Here's an illustration of how to navigate the Activity app using the Motion Pointer:

1. Double-press the side button while the watch face is displayed and the Apple Watch is in list view to activate AssistiveTouch.

2. Double-squeeze once more to bring up the Action Menu, touch to navigate to the "Press Crown" action, and then double-squeeze to select it.

3. If the Activity app is not already open, pinch or double-pinch to advance forward or backward, and then squeeze to open it.

4. Double-tap to open the Action Menu, pinch to locate the Interaction action, and then select it by double-tapping again.
   Motion Pointer must be selected.

5. To activate the Motion Pointer, press down on it.
   A cursor appears on the screen.

6. To scroll down, tilt the watch until the cursor reaches the bottom of the display. To access the Sharing interface, place the cursor on the right edge and swipe to the right.

7. Hold the cursor over an icon for a brief period of time to select it.

8. To return to the watch face, double-press the button to open the Action Menu, touch to select the Press Crown

action, and then double-press the button once more to execute it.

Use rapid actions

When your Apple Watch displays a notification, you can take immediate action to address it. When an incoming call arrives, for instance, a prompt indicates that you can double-pinch to answer it. Quick actions can also be used to snooze an alarm or stop a timer, initiate a workout when Apple Watch detects activity that appears to be a workout, or take a picture when the Camera app's viewfinder and shutter button are visible. Follow these steps to enable or disable fast actions.

1. Launch the Apple Watch Settings application.
2. Navigate to Accessibility > Quick Actions and select one of the available options.

You can choose to have fast actions available at all times, only when AssistiveTouch is enabled, or not at all. You can also select Full appearance, which displays a banner and highlights the action button, or Minimal appearance, which only displays the button (the action button is highlighted without a banner).

Tap "Try it out" to experiment with the rapid actions gesture.

Change the AssistiveTouch parameters.

You can alter what happens when you pinch, clench, or use the Motion Pointer, as well as the Motion Pointer's sensitivity.

Launch the Settings application on your Apple Watch, navigate to Accessibility > AssistiveTouch, and then perform one of the following:

- You can modify the behavior of gestures by selecting Hand Gestures, tapping a gesture, and then selecting an action or Siri shortcut.

- Customize the Motion Pointer: Tap Motion Pointer, then modify the sensitivity, activation time, movement tolerance, and hot edge parameters.

- Choose between Automatic and Manual scanning styles. Using Automatic, actions are highlighted sequentially. Manual allows you to switch between actions by gesturing.

- Appearance: Activate High Contrast to make the highlight stand out more, and tap Color to alter the highlight's color.

- Customize Menu: Add your preferred actions, relocate and resize the Action Menu, and adjust its auto-scrolling speed.

- Confirm with AssistiveTouch: Activate AssistiveTouch to use it to confirm payments with the passcode or whenever double-clicking the side button is required.

Additionally, you can launch the Apple Watch app on your iPhone, select My Watch, then navigate to Accessibility > AssistiveTouch.

Use VoiceOver with a Bluetooth keyboard on Apple Watch

Bluetooth keyboards can be used to control VoiceOver output. To use Apple Watch with VoiceOver, hold down the appropriate modifier keys and type.

Put a Bluetooth keyboard in position.

1. On the Apple Watch, launch the Settings application .
2. Click Accessibility followed by VoiceOver and Keyboards.
3. Scroll to the bottom of the screen and then tap the keyboard under Devices.

Change the keyboard settings.

1. On the Apple Watch, launch the Settings application.
2. Click Accessibility followed by VoiceOver and Keyboards.
3. Select one of these:

Setting	Description
Phonetic feedback	Choose to hear characters and phonetics or phonetics only.
Typing feedback	Choose to hear characters, words, or characters and words as you type on the Bluetooth keyboard.
Modifier keys	Choose the modifier keys that must be pressed on a hardware keyboard to activate VoiceOver key commands. Options are Control + Option and Caps Lock.
Keyboard interaction time	Set the amount of time to wait before VoiceOver can start Slide to Type or make use of alternative keys on the software keyboard. Use the plus and minus buttons to adjust interaction time from zero to four seconds.

Use the keyboard to move around.

Use the following keys on a Bluetooth keyboard to navigate.

Setting	Action
Right Arrow key	Move to next item.
Left Arrow key	Move to previous item.
Modifier key + Down Arrow key	Read out character or phonetics of selected item from left to right.
Modifier key + Up Arrow key	Read out character or phonetics of selected item from right to left.
Modifier key + Space bar	Tap selected item.

Zoom with the Apple Watch.

Utilize Zoom to enlarge the Apple Watch display.

Zoom Initiate

1. On the Apple Watch, launch the Settings application.
2. Go to Accessibility > Zoom and activate it.

The ability to zoom in and out

Once Zoom is enabled, you can perform the aforementioned actions with your Apple Watch.

- To zoom in or out, double-tap the Apple Watch screen with two fingers.

Tip: When configuring your Apple Watch, double-tap with two fingers for a clearer view.

- Move around (pan): Drag the screen with two fingertips or rotate the Digital Crown to pan left to right and up and down across the entire page. The small Zoom icon that appears shows you where you are on the page.

- Use the Digital Crown normally instead of panning: Tap the screen once with two fingers to alternate between using the Digital Crown to pan and the way it functions when Zoom is turned off (for example, to scroll a list or zoom a map).

- To adjust the magnification, double-tap and hold two fingers on the screen, then drag your fingers up or down. Tap the plus or minus icon on the Maximum Zoom Level slider to limit the magnification.

The Apple Watch lets you feel the time.

Apple Watch can display the time on your wrist with a series of distinct touches when in silent mode.

1. On the Apple Watch, launch the Settings application .
2. Tap Clock, then navigate to the bottom and tap Taptic Time.
3. Select Digits, Terse, or Morse Code as the setting for Taptic Time. Hours and minutes are displayed as follows:

- Digits: The Apple Watch performs a long tap every 10 hours, followed by a short tap every hour, a long tap every 10 minutes, and a short tap every minute thereafter.

- Short: The Apple Watch taps long every five hours, short every hour thereafter, and long every quarter hour.
- The Apple Watch displays the time in Morse code when each number is tapped.

4. Feel the time by placing two fingertips on the watch face and holding them there.

Even if the Always On Display is dimmed, Taptic Time continues to function.

Additionally, you can set up Taptic Time on your iPhone. Open the Apple Watch app on your iPhone, select My Watch, then navigate to Clock > Taptic Time to activate Taptic Time.

Taptic Time will not function if your Apple Watch is set to always display the current time. Go to Settings > Clock and enable Control with Silent Mode under Speak Time to enable Taptic Time.

Apple Watch allows you to adjust the text size and other visual settings.

You can adjust the text size and other settings to make it simpler to interact with the screen.

Modify text size

1. Touch and hold the bottom of the screen, then swipe up.

2. Simply press ^{A}A and rotate the Digital Crown to make adjustments.

You can choose how text and other things appear.

You can change how things appear on the screen by making text bold, using grayscale, and setting other options. Open the Settings app on your Apple Watch, select Accessibility, and toggle the following options on or off:

- Stop/Go Labels

  If you enable button labels, you will see a one (1) next to any active option and a zero (0) next to any inactive option.
- Tonal range
- Make things less transparent
- With some backgrounds, reducing transparency makes text simpler to read.
- Text in italics

Additionally, you can launch the Apple Watch app on your iPhone, tap My Watch, tap Accessibility, and then modify a setting.

Note: Bold text and grayscale adjustments will not take effect until the Apple Watch is restarted.

Reduce animation

You can control the movement of the Home Screen and the opening and closing of applications.

1. On the Apple Watch, launch the Settings application .
2. To enable Reduce Motion, navigate to Accessibility > Reduce Motion.

Additionally, you can launch the Apple Watch app on your iPhone, tap My Watch, navigate to Accessibility > Reduce Motion, and enable Reduce Motion.

Tip: When you set on Reduce Motion and choose grid view for the Home Screen, all app icons are the same size.

Adjust Apple Watch settings for motor skills

You can modify how the touchscreen responds to inputs if you cannot figure out how to use it.

Set the pace via the button on the side

1. On the Apple Watch, launch the Settings application.
2. Navigate to Accessibility > Side Button > tempo, and then select a tempo.

You can also access Accessibility > Side Button Click Speed by opening the Apple Watch app on your iPhone, tapping My Watch, and then selecting Accessibility > Side Button Click Speed.

Employ Touch Arrangements.

1. On the Apple Watch, launch the Settings application
2. To perform the aforementioned actions, navigate to Accessibility > Touch Accommodations.
- React to touches that last for a certain amount of time: Turn on Hold Duration, and then use the plus and minus buttons to alter how long the hold will last.
- To use swipe gestures without having to wait the specified period of time, tap Swipe Gestures and then toggle Swipe

Gestures on. You can determine the distance required before a sweep gesture begins.

- To disregard multiple touches, toggle Ignore Repeat and then use the plus and minus controls to adjust the interval between touches. Then, if you contact the screen rapidly more than once, your Apple Watch will interpret it as a single touch.

- Use the location where you touched first or last: Use the location where you touched first or last.

If you choose Use Initial Touch Location, your Apple Watch uses the place where you first touched it, like when you touched an app on the Home Screen. If you select Use Final Touch Location, your watch will capture the tap at the location where your finger is lifted. Apple Watch will respond to a contact if the user removes their finger from the display within a predetermined amount of time. Tap the plus or minus icon to modify the timing. If you wait longer than the gesture delay, other gestures, such as dragging, will be recognized by your device.

Additionally, you can launch the Apple Watch application on your iPhone, select My Watch, and then navigate to Accessibility > Touch Accommodations.

Configure and use RTT on Apple Watch (cellular models only).

Real-time text (RTT) is a protocol that transmits audio while text is being typed. If you have difficulty hearing or speaking, an Apple

Watch with cellular can use RTT to communicate with you when you're away from your iPhone if you have hearing or speech impairments. Apple Watch includes Software RTT, which can be configured in the Apple Watch app. It requires no additional devices.

Important: RTT is not supported by all carriers or locations. When an Apple Watch user in the United States makes an emergency call, special characters or tones are transmitted to the operator. The operator may or may not be able to hear or respond to these tones, depending on their location. Apple does not guarantee that the operator will receive or acknowledge an RTT call.

Activate RTT

1. On your iPhone, launch the Apple Watch application.
2. Tap "My Watch," then navigate to "Accessibility" and "RTT." Then, toggle "RTT" on.
3. Tap Relay Number, then enter the phone number you would like to use for RTT relay communications.
4. Enable transmit Immediately to transmit every character as it is typed. Disable to transmit only completed messages.

Dial the RTT number.

1. Open the Phone app on the Apple Watch.
2. Touch "Contacts," then navigate with the Digital Crown.
3. select the desired contact, then scroll down and select the RTT button.

4. Write a message by hand, select a response from a drop-down menu, or send an emoji.

However, not all languages are supported by Scribble.

Similar to Messages, text can be viewed on an Apple Watch.

You will be informed if the individual you are calling does not have RTT enabled.

Respond to a call from RTT

1. When you hear or sense the call alert, raise your wrist to see who is calling.
2. Tap the Answer icon, then scroll to the bottom and tap the RTT button.
3. Write a message by hand, select a response from a drop-down menu, or send an emoji.

However, not all languages are supported by Scribble.

Edit standard responses

When making or receiving an RTT call on Apple Watch, you can respond with a single tap. Follow these procedures to generate more of your own responses:

1. On your iPhone, launch the Apple Watch application.
2. Tap "My Watch," then "Accessibility," "RTT," and "Default Replies."
3. Tap "Add reply," type your response, and then tap "Done."

Most responses conclude with "GA," which stands for "go ahead" and indicates that you are ready to hear what the other individual has to say.

Tap Edit on the Default Replies screen to modify existing responses, discard them, or rearrange them.

Apple Watch audio settings are easy.

If you want to hear a signal from both the left and right audio channels when you connect your Apple Watch to speakers or headphones, activate Mono Audio. On your Apple Watch, you can also adjust the proportion between the left and right audio channels. And you can modify AirPods' configuration to make them simpler to use.

Adjust the mono audio settings and the equilibrium.

Launch the Settings app on your Apple Watch, tap Accessibility, and then, under Hearing, select one of the following options:

- Change the sound from stereo to mono.
- Modify the sound balance by tapping the L or R icon under Mono Audio.

You can also modify the audio balance by opening the Apple Watch app on your iPhone, tapping My Watch, tapping Accessibility, then tapping Mono Audio.

Change AirPods configuration

You can adjust how quickly you press and how long you press and hold on your Apple Watch-compatible AirPods. On AirPods Pro, it is also possible to activate noise cancellation for use with a single AirPod.

1. On the Apple Watch, launch the Settings application .
2. Select your AirPods and then tap Settings under Accessibility > AirPods.

Additionally, you can access the Apple Watch application on your iPhone, tap My Watch, and then navigate to Accessibility > AirPods.

Listen to the HomePod recording

When the HomePod and Apple Watch share the same Apple ID, HomePod announcements can be typed on the Apple Watch.

1. On the Apple Watch, launch the Settings application .
2. Go to Accessibility and enable Show Audio Subtitles.

Siri provides access to Apple Watch's accessibility features.

Siri is frequently the easiest method to begin using the accessibility features of your Apple Watch. You can use Siri to activate apps, turn on or off many settings, or use Siri to do what it does best: be your smart personal assistant.

Siri: Say "Turn VoiceOver on" and "Turn VoiceOver off."

Siri knows when VoiceOver is enabled, so it will frequently provide additional information. Additionally, VoiceOver can read aloud what Siri displays on the screen.

You can specify how long Siri should wait for you to complete speaking.

1. On the Apple Watch, launch the Settings application ⚙.
2. Click Accessibility > Siri, then tap Default, Longer, or Longest beneath Siri Pause Time.

Instead of speaking, you can dictate to Siri.

You do not need to speak to Siri in order to use it. Follow these instructions to type Siri commands rather than voice them.

1. On the Apple Watch, launch the Settings application.
2. Navigate to Accessibility > Siri and enable Type to Siri.

Shortcut for accessibility on Apple Watch

You can toggle the following accessibility features with a triple-click on the Digital Crown: AssistiveTouch, Control Nearby Devices, Left/Right Balance, Reduce Motion, Reduce Transparency, Touch Accommodations, VoiceOver, and Zoom.

Install the Accessibility Shortcut.

1. On the Apple Watch, launch the Settings application.
2. Accessibility > Accessibility Shortcut, then select one or more of the options available.

Alternatively, you can open the Apple Watch app on your iPhone, touch My Watch, navigate to Accessibility > Accessibility Shortcut, and then select an option.

Take the shorter route.

Rapidly press the Digital Crown three times.

1. If you configured the shortcut to activate or deactivate multiple features, select the desired feature, then tap Done.
2. Click the Digital Crown three times again to turn off the feature that makes the game simpler to use.

Restart the Apple Watch

If something isn't functioning properly, restart your Apple Watch and the iPhone with which it is paired.

Launch the Apple Watch.

- To power off your Apple Watch, press and drag the Power Off slider to the right while holding down the side button until the sliders appear.
- Press and hold the side button until the Apple logo appears to activate the Apple Watch.

Note: While your Apple Watch is charging, it cannot be turned back on.

Start the iPhone that was paired.

- Stop using your iPhone: For Face ID-enabled models, press and hold the side button and a volume button, and then drag the selector to the right. For devices without Face ID, press and hold the top or side button until the slider appears, then drag it to the right. Additionally, you can close down any model by selecting Settings > General > close Down.
- To activate the iPhone, press and hold the side or upper button until the Apple logo appears.

Start Apple Watch from scratch

If you are unable to power off your Apple Watch or the issue persists, you may need to restart it. This should only be performed if you are unable to reset your Apple Watch.

To force restart, simultaneously press and hold the side button and the Digital Crown for at least ten seconds, until the Apple logo appears.

Remove your Apple Watch

Forgetting your passcode may necessitate erasing your Apple Watch's memory.

Delete Apple Watch and configurations

1. On your Apple Watch, launch "Settings."
2. Tap Erase All Content and Settings after navigating to Settings > General > Reset and entering your passcode.

You have two options if you have a cellular plan for your Apple Watch: Erase All or Erase All and Keep Plan. Select Erase

Everything to erase everything from your Apple Watch. Select Erase Everything & Retain Plan if you wish to expunge everything and then reattach it to your cell phone plan.

Additionally, you can open the Apple Watch application on your iPhone, press My Watch, navigate to General > Reset, and tap Erase Apple Watch Content and Settings.

If you forgot your passcode and can't get into the Settings app on your Apple Watch, place it on its charger and press and hold the side button until the sliders show up. Hold down the Digital Crown button and then select the Reset button.

Note: Activation Lock is enabled when Apple Watch is erased in this manner. With Activation Lock, if your Apple Watch is lost or stolen, no one else will be able to use it.

After the reset has been completed and your Apple Watch has restarted, you will need to re-pair it with your iPhone. Launch the Apple Watch application on your iPhone, and then follow the on-screen instructions on both your iPhone and Apple Watch.

Delete your mobile phone subscription.

If you have an Apple Watch with cellular, you can terminate your cell plan at any time.

1. On your iPhone, launch the Apple Watch application.

2. Tap My Watch, then Cellular, then tap ⓘ alongside your cellular plan.

3. Tap Remove [carrier's name] Plan, then affirm your selection.

You may need to contact your carrier if you wish to remove this Apple Watch from your cellular plan.

Get back the Apple Watch

If your Apple Watch displays an animation of a watch and an iPhone being brought near together, proceed as follows:

1. Place the iPhone near the Apple Watch.
   iOS 15 must be installed on your iPhone.
   4.x or later, Wi-Fi connectivity, Bluetooth activation, and unlocking are required.
2. Place your Apple device on its charger.
3. Double-click the side button on your Apple Watch, and then follow the instructions presented on your iPhone.

Restore an Apple Watch from its backup

Your associated iPhone backs up your Apple Watch automatically, and you can restore it from a previously saved backup. When you back up your iPhone to iCloud, your Mac, or your PC, the Apple Watch is also backed up. You cannot view the information contained in your iCloud-stored backups.

Apple Watch backups and resets are possible.

- Save your Apple Watch: When an Apple Watch is paired with an iPhone, the content of the Apple Watch is automatically stored up to the iPhone. Before the devices are unpaired, a backup is created.

- Restore your Apple Watch from a backup: You can choose "Restore from Backup" and choose a previously stored backup on your iPhone when pairing your Apple Watch with the same iPhone again or when buying a new Apple Watch.

A managed Apple Watch automatically backs up to a family member's iCloud account while it is both powered on and connected to a Wi-Fi network. Turn off iCloud Backups by opening the Settings app on the controlled Apple Watch, going to [account name] > iCloud, and then selecting iCloud Backups.

Apple Watch software update

You can look for software updates for your Apple Watch by using the Apple Watch app on your iPhone.

Check for and apply software update patches

1. On your iPhone, launch the Apple Watch application.
2. after choosing "My Watch," choose "General" and "Software Update." When an update is available, choose "Download and Install."

On your Apple Watch, you may also open the Settings app and go to General > Software Update.

If you neglect the passcode for your Apple Watch, you will be unable to access it.

If your Apple Watch is disabled because you forget your passcode or entered it incorrectly too many times, the Apple Watch app on your iPhone will allow you to re-enter the passcode. If you still cannot remember your passcode, you can reset and re-configure your Apple Watch.

Important: If Erase Data is enabled, your Apple Watch's data will be deleted after 10 unsuccessful passcode attempts.

Important safety information for Apple Watch

WARNING: If you disregard these safety instructions, you could start a fire, receive an electric charge, injure yourself, or damage your Apple Watch or other items. Before using Apple Watch, please review the following safety information.

Handing Care should be taken with the Apple Watch. Apple Watch cases are manufactured of a variety of materials, including:

- The Apple Watch case is composed of 7000 series aluminum, Ion-X glass, and a composite rear (plastic). The Apple Watch case is composed of ceramic on both the rear and front.
- The rear of the Apple Watch case is composed of ceramic, sapphire, and titanium.
- The rear of the Apple Watch case is constructed of ceramic.

Apple Watch contains fragile electronic components that are susceptible to damage if dropped, burned, poked, or compressed. If you drop or strike your Apple Watch with sufficient force, the ceramic case may chip or shatter. It is dangerous to use a damaged Apple Watch, such as one with a fractured screen or case, a liquid leak, or a broken band. Avoid large quantities of dust or sediment.

Repairing Do not disassemble your Apple Watch and do not attempt to repair it yourself. If you disassemble an Apple Watch, you could potentially damage it, loose its water resistance, or injure yourself. If your Apple Watch is damaged or malfunctioning, contact Apple or an Apple-authorized service provider. At support.apple.com/watch/repair/service, you can obtain additional information regarding service.

Battery Don't attempt to replace the Apple Watch's battery on your own. You could cause the battery to overcharge, which could be harmful to you. The lithium-ion battery in an Apple Watch should only be repaired by Apple or an Apple-approved service provider. When ordering battery service, you may receive a replacement Apple Watch instead of your original. Batteries must be recycled or discarded in a manner distinct from other waste. Do not ignite the battery.

Distraction Using Apple Watch in certain situations can distract you from what you're doing, which can be hazardous (avoid reading a text message while driving, for example). Follow the rules that prohibit you from using your phone or restrict its use.

Navigation Maps, directions, and applications that function based on your location require data services. These data services are subject to change and may not be accessible in all locations. This means that maps, directions, and other information based on your current location may be unavailable, incorrect, or absent. Location Services is required for certain Maps functions. If there are discrepancies between the information on your Apple Watch and what you see around you, look at the signs. Use these services only when you can devote your entire attention to them. Always obey signs, laws, and rules wherever you use Apple Watch, and always use common sense.

Charging Apple Watch can be charged with an Apple-made magnetic charging accessory and an Apple-made power adapter (each sold separately). You can also charge your Apple Watch with a power adapter from a third-party company as long as it functions with USB 2.0 or later and meets safety standards in your country and internationally. Other adapters may not meet safety standards, so charging with them could be harmful or fatal.

Using damaged cables or chargers or charging when there is moisture can cause a fire, an electric shock, bodily harm, or damage to your Apple Watch or other items. If you wish to charge your Apple Watch using a magnetic charging cable or dock and a power adapter, ensure that the cable or dock is entirely inserted into the adapter before plugging the adapter into an outlet. It is essential to use or charge Apple Watch, the magnetic charging accessory, and the power adapter in a well-ventilated area.

Long-term exposure Apple Watch, Apple Watch magnetic charging accessories, and the power adapter all meet the surface temperature limits established by international and regional safety standards and the legislation of the country in which they are used when subjected to prolonged heat. However, even within these parameters, prolonged contact with heated surfaces can cause pain or discomfort. Apple Watch, magnetic charging accoutrements for Apple Watch, and power adapter will become warm when connected to a power source. Using cellular on an Apple Watch Series 3 (GPS + Cellular), Apple Watch Series 4 (GPS + Cellular), Apple Watch Series 5 (GPS + Cellular), Apple Watch SE (GPS + Cellular), Apple Watch Series 6 (GPS + Cellular), Apple Watch Series 7 (GPS + Cellular), Apple Watch SE (2nd Generation, GPS + Cellular), or Apple Watch Series 8 (GPS + Cellular) may cause the watch to become warm. Employ common sense to prevent prolonged skin contact with the Apple Watch, Apple Watch magnetic charging accessories, and the power adapter when they are inserted in. For instance, do not lie on or place your Apple Watch under a blanket, pillow, or your body while it is charging or while its magnetic charging accessories or power adapter are plugged into a power source. If you have a health condition that makes it difficult for you to sense heat against your body, take extra precautions. If the Apple Watch becomes too heated, remove it.

Hearing loss Listening to harsh sounds could damage your hearing. Sounds can seem quieter than they really are if there is a lot of background commotion or if you keep listening to loud music. Before inserting a Bluetooth-enabled headset into your ear, activate audio playback and verify the volume.

WARNING: If you listen at loud volumes for an extended period of time, you may damage your hearing.

Exposure to radio frequency Apple Watch connects to wireless networks using radio waves. Open the Apple Watch app on your iPhone, tap My Watch, then tap General > About > Legal > RF Exposure or go to apple.com/legal/rfexposure for information about radio frequency (RF) energy that comes from radio signals and steps you can take to limit your exposure.

Radio frequency interference Pay attention to signs and notices that prohibit or restrict the use of electronic devices. Even though the Apple Watch and its magnetic charging accessories are designed, tested, and manufactured to comply with radio frequency emission regulations, these emissions can interfere with the operation of other electronic devices and cause them to fail. Unplug any magnetic charging accoutrements for your Apple Watch, and turn it off or into airplane mode when it's not permitted to be used, such as on an airplane or when instructed by the police.

Interference with medical devices Some Apple Watch bands and magnetic charging accoutrements contain radios and/or components that emit electromagnetic fields. These magnets and electromagnetic fields may interfere with certain medical equipment.

Consult your physician and the manufacturer of your medical device to determine if you must maintain a safe distance between your medical device and your Apple Watch, its bands, or its magnetic charging accessories. Frequently, manufacturers will provide instructions on how to use their products around wireless or magnetic devices without causing interference. If you believe that the Apple Watch, some of the bands, and the magnetic charging accoutrements for the Apple Watch are interfering with your medical device, you should stop using them.

Implanted pacemakers and defibrillators may contain sensors that respond to magnets and radios when they are nearby. Keep your Apple Watch, some of the bands, and any magnetic charging accessories for your Apple Watch at a safe distance (more than 6 inches/15 cm, but verify with your doctor and the company that made your device for specific instructions) to avoid any potential issues.

Apple Watch is not a medical device, and it should not be used as a substitute for a doctor's advice. It is neither designed nor intended for use in diagnosing disease or other conditions, nor in curing, treating, mitigating the effects of, or preventing any disease or condition. Before making any health-related decisions, please consult your doctor or nurse.

Medical conditions Consult your physician prior to beginning or modifying an Apple Watch exercise regimen. When exercising, use caution and pay close attention to your surroundings. Stop exercising immediately if you experience pain or if you feel faint, dazed, exhausted, or short of breath. By exercising, you acknowledge all associated risks, including the possibility of injury.

Consult your physician before using Apple Watch if you have a medical condition that may be affected by it, such as seizures, blackouts, eyestrain, or migraines.

Explosive weather and other types of weather It may be unsafe to charge or use an Apple Watch in an area where the air contains a high concentration of flammable compounds, vapors, or particles (such as grain, dust, or metal powders) that could cause an explosion. If you put your Apple Watch in a place where there are a lot of industrial chemicals, like near-evaporating liquid gases like helium, it could get damaged or cease working. Follow all notices and instructions.

High-stakes activities Apple Watch is not intended for use in situations where its failure could result in death, grievous injury, or damage to the environment.

Choking hazard Some Apple Watch bands could pose a choking hazard for young children. Keep young children away from these groups.

Skin sensitivities Some individuals with skin sensitivities may experience reactions to the materials used in jewelry, watches, and other items worn near to the skin for extended periods of time. This can occur due to allergies, the environment, prolonged contact with irritants such as soap or perspiration, or another factor. If you have allergies or other sensitivities, you may be more likely to experience discomfort from a wearable device. If you have sensitive epidermis, please exercise extra caution when wearing an Apple Watch. If you wear your Apple Watch too snugly, it may become more irritating. Remove your Apple Watch periodically to allow your epidermis to breathe. Maintaining a clean and dry Apple Watch and band will reduce the likelihood of skin irritation. If the skin around or under your Apple Watch becomes red, distended, itchy, or in any other way painful, please remove it and consult a physician before reapplying it. If you continue to use it after the symptoms have subsided, the irritation could return or worsen.

Some Apple Watch models with an aluminum or stainless steel case, the stainless steel components of some Apple Watch bands, the metal components of Hermès bands, and the watch and band magnets all contain nickel. Nickel exposure from these materials is unlikely, but nickel-allergic individuals should be cautious until they are certain they are not experiencing a reaction.

Apple Watch's case and bands contain trace quantities of acrylates and methacrylates. Acrylates and methacrylates are found in numerous skin-contact products, such as bandages. Some individuals may be allergic to them, or they may develop an allergy over time. The Apple Watch and its bands are constructed so that acrylates and methacrylates do not come into contact with the epidermis.

Apple Watch and its bands are manufactured from materials that comply with U.S. jewelry standards. Consumer Product Safety Commission, European Union, and other international groups.

A lost Apple Watch can be sold, given away, or kept safe.

Be sure to disconnect your Apple Watch from your iPhone before selling or donating it. This deletes everything on the device, including payment cards, and removes the Activation Lock (which inhibits unauthorized use). If you lose your Apple Watch, you can activate "lost mode" on it.

Disable Activation Lock and detach Apple Watch

1. On your iPhone, launch the Apple Watch application.
2. Click My Watch, followed by All Watches.
3. Touch your Apple Watch, followed by "Unpair Apple Watch."

The Apple Watch is removed from your iCloud account and the Activation Lock is removed.

Find your missing Apple Watch.

1. On your iPhone, launch the Apple Watch application.
2. Click My Watch, followed by All Watches.
3. Touch ⓘ your Apple Watch, followed by "Find My Apple Watch."
4. In the Find My app on your iPhone, you can tap your watch to view its location on a map.

If the map indicates that your Apple Watch is where you are, tap Play Sound.

Mark your Apple Watch as misplaced

When you report your Apple Watch as missing, it is secured with a passcode to prevent unauthorized access to your personal data. Also, you can't use credit or debit cards in Wallet to pay with Apple Pay.

1. On your iPhone, launch the Apple Watch application.

2. Click My Watch, followed by All Watches.

3. Touch ⓘ your Apple Watch, followed by "Find My Apple Watch."

4. Open the Find My app on your iPhone and tap Activate under "Mark as Lost." Then, select "Continue."

5. If you want to be contacted if someone finds your Apple Watch, enter a phone number.

6. Tap Next, then enter a message to be displayed on your Apple Watch if it is found.

7. Tap "Enable" to report a missing Apple Watch.

When you locate your Apple Watch, you can either enter its passcode or use your iPhone to open locate My, tap Devices, tap your Apple Watch, tap Activated, and then tap Turn Off Mark as Lost.

Eliminate a misplaced Apple Watch.

Before erasing your device, search for it or play a sound on it. After deletion, neither option is available with Find My.

1. On your iPhone, launch the Apple Watch application.

2. Click My Watch, followed by All Watches.

3. Touch ⓘ your Apple Watch, followed by "Find My Apple Watch."

4. select the watch within the Find My iPhone app, and then select Erase This Device.

It is possible to discard credit cards using a web browser.

If your Apple Watch is lost or stolen, you can remove your cards by signing in with your Apple ID at appleid.apple.com.

1. Select the desired device from the Devices section.
2. To remove all cards from Apple Pay, select "Remove all cards."

You may also contact your card issuers.

If your iPhone and Apple Watch are no longer working together or one of them isn't functioning as it should, delete everything from your Apple Watch and then use the Apple Watch app (if available) on your iPhone to unpair it.

Made in United States
North Haven, CT
06 December 2023

45176015R00187